D1340052

SECRET
CAPE TOWN

Justin Fox, Alison Westwood and Lesley Cox

JONGLEZ PUBLISHING

Travel guides

Alison Westwood grew up in Johannesburg, but was fortunate enough to find her way to Cape Town in 1999. She immediately decided that it was the best city in the world. Although she's travelled extensively on five continents since then, she hasn't yet found any reason to change that opinion. Alison has a degree in journalism from Rhodes University and has worked as a travel writer and photographer for print and online publications for more than a decade. Her preference for the unusual, the interesting, and the just plain odd made the task of tracking down Cape Town's untold secrets particularly exciting and, if possible, made her love her adoptive home even more.

Justin Fox is an award-winning writer and photographer based in Cape Town. He's a former editor of *Getaway International* travel magazine. Justin was a Rhodes Scholar and received a doctorate in English from Oxford University after which he became a research fellow at the University of Cape Town, where he now teaches part time. His articles and photographs have appeared internationally in a number of publications and on a wide range of topics, while his short stories and poems have appeared in various anthologies. He is a two-time Mondi journalism award winner.

Lesley Cox grew up in England, and after earning a degree in Industrial Biology, she joined a multinational company involved with medical equipment, spending just over a decade travelling the world for both personal and work purposes. In 1995, this career brought her to South Africa, where she immediately decided it would become her home. For the last 20 years, Lesley has led private day tours of Cape Town, and after graduating in 2016 with an Honours Degree in History, she now specialises in the history and heritage of Cape Town through walking tours for locals and visitors. In her spare time, she is involved with a variety of heritage projects through museums and non-profit enterprises.

We immensely enjoyed writing the *Secret Cape Town* guide and hope that, like us, you will continue to discover the unusual, secret and lesser-known facets of this city. Accompanying the description of some sites, you will find historical information and anecdotes that will let you understand the city in all its complexity.

Secret Cape Town also sheds light on the numerous yet overlooked details of places we pass by every day. These details are an invitation to pay more attention to the urban landscape and, more generally, to regard our city with the same curiosity and attention we often feel when travelling ...

Comments on this guide and its contents, as well as information on sites not mentioned, are welcome and will help us to enrich future editions.

Don't hesitate to contact us:
• Jonglez Publishing,
   25, rue du Maréchal Foch
   78000 Versailles, France
• Email: info@jonglezpublishing.com

p. 70
p. 122
p. 12
p. 180

Philadelphia

Duynefontein

Melkbosstrand

Robben Island

Bloubergstrand

Table Bay

Green Point

Sea Point

City Bowl

Table Mountain

ATLANTIC OCEAN

1 000 m

851 m

742 m

514 m

594 m

Hout Bay

928 m

Duikerpunt

Noordhoek

Chapman's Bay

Kommetjie

Fish Hoek

Ocean View

390 m

Simon's Town

576 m

Cape of Good Hope

Cape Point

Muizenberg

Seal Island

Plumstead

Athlone

Bellvill

Cape Town International Airport

Philippi

Strandfontein

N

0   5   10 km

CONTENTS

City Bowl

Atlantic Seabord

Southern Suburbs

CONTENTS

South Peninsula

West Coast & Cape Flats

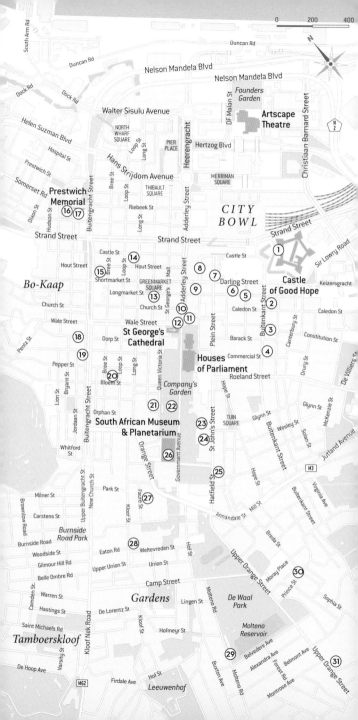

City Bowl

GREAT WAR MEMORIAL

An oak cross from Delville Wood in France

To the left of the main entrance to the Castle of Good Hope

On the outer curtain wall of the Castle of Good Hope is a cross fashioned out of oak from the forest at Delville (northern France), where a great many South African soldiers lost their lives during the Battle of Delville Wood.

The simple memorial sits in a white, pedimented alcove with an inscription that reads: "In memory of the officers and all other ranks of the 1st (Cape) Regiment of the South African Infantry (Overseas) Brigade who fell in the Great War 1914–1918. This cross was first erected in France by their surviving comrades."

The Battle of Delville Wood lives in South African memory as one of the bloodiest ever fought by the nation's soldiers. As part of the 9th (Scottish) Division, 1 SA Brigade fought in the Somme offensive of 1916, particularly the battles of Trones Wood, Berfnay Wood, Longueval and Delville Wood. The SA Brigade was almost entirely wiped out in this offensive: out of approximately 4,000 men who started the battle, only 29 officers and 751 troops survived.

Delville Wood (Bois d'Elville) was a thick tangle of trees, chiefly beech and hornbeam (the forest was later replanted with oak and birch by the South African government). As part of a general offensive beginning on 14 July, General Douglas Haig, commander of the British Expeditionary Force, intended to capture the German position between Delville Wood and Bazentin le Petit.

The 1st SA Infantry Brigade made its Western Front début here and captured Delville Wood on 15 July. The South Africans held the position until 19 July at great cost. When captured, the village and wood formed a salient, which could be fired on by German artillery from three sides. For the rest of July and August, both sides fought for control of the wood and village but neither achieved a decisive victory.

A Two-Minute Silence Originated in Cape Town

The idea of a two-minute silence to commemorate those who fell in World War One began in Cape Town. When the noonday gun was fired from Signal Hill on 14 May 1918 it brought the city to a dead stop for two minutes: one minute for those who died, one minute for the survivors. The two-minute silence has been observed internationally since 1919 at 11am on 11 November and Remembrance Sunday each year.

OLD GRANARY BUILDING

An historic building with a chequered past

Buitenkant Street
tutu.org.za

The Old Granary building, left vacant and neglected for more than a decade, is scarcely noticed by most passersby, yet it is one of the most important architectural sites in the city. Dating back to 1814, it was originally built as a customs house. It's had a particularly chequered past, being used as a police court, a granary, a post office, a women's prison, the Civil Engineers' office and Cape Town's first (informal) astronomical observatory. Built in a neo-classical style, it's also a rare surviving example of a city building worked on by slaves.

Designed by the French-born architect Louis Michel Thibault, who worked on many of Cape Town's most important buildings of the time, it was one of the last buildings Thibault helped to plan before he died of pneumonia in 1815. The German sculptor Anton Anreith, one of South Africa's greatest craftsmen, who worked closely with Thibault on many projects, created the pediment featuring the British coat of arms and figures of Britannia and Neptune on the building's corners.

As a women's prison, it was a grim place, described by at least one of its inmates as a "den of infamy". On a happier note, it provided a first base

for Fearon Fallows, a young Cambridge astronomer sent to Cape Town in 1820 to establish an observatory. When he arrived, the authorities refused to pay his expenses or give him anywhere to store his instruments. In fact, the ship's captain would have dumped them on the beach had the Burgher Senate not intervened and given him a room in the Old Granary.

With a R36 million investment on renovations, today The Old Granary is leased to the Desmond & Leah Tutu Legacy Foundation, for their office, a small museum and exhibitions.

NEARBY
The Lion and the Unicorn
At the back of the Slave Lodge, on the side of the building facing Parliament Street, is another pediment with a British coat of arms sculpted by Anreith, apparently in the same year. The story goes that Anreith kept this work hidden until its unveiling, when the British must have been shocked to discover that instead of the usual proud heraldic supporters on either side, it depicted a sad and downcast lion and a very distressed-looking unicorn. When asked for an explanation, Anreith said it symbolised Britain after years of fighting the Napoleonic wars. Somewhat surprisingly, the British permitted the piece to remain in place – a lesson, perhaps, to modern South Africans, who have become fond of pulling down unpopular statues.

SEVEN STEPS REMAINING FLAGSTONES

A powerful symbol of diversity and inclusivity

District Six Museum
25A Buitenkant Street
021-466-7200
info@districtsix.co.za
Monday–Saturday 9am–4pm

Located at the intersection of Hanover Street and Horsburg Lane, neither of which remain today, the Seven Steps were a famous meeting point as well as a place for youths and gangs to hang out. Hanover Street was the main thoroughfare of the lively, mixed community of District Six and the steps were its symbolic heart.

Inhabitants of the suburb were forcibly removed under the draconian Group Areas Act of the apartheid regime, which saw coloured people ousted from the city centre in the late 1960s and 70s. Apart from a few places of worship, almost the entire suburb was bulldozed. Even the old streets were erased.

The spot where the Seven Steps once stood lies close to the intersection of Tennant Street and Keizersgracht, within the grounds of CPUT. But there is nothing there to remind one of the old meeting place.

To find the last remains of the Seven Steps, visit the District Six Museum. On the second floor there's an alcove with two flagstones said to be from the original steps. Surrounding them is a display of photographs and paintings that depict the vibrant street life of this area. They give an impression of the bustling community, family homes above colourful shopfronts, draped laundry, rolling trams and people lingering on the pavements.

District Six was Cape Town's own Harlem and one of the first settlements for freed urban slaves after emancipation. The suburb represented a coming together of all races and creeds and saw the creolisation of local cultures. As such, it was a threat to the apartheid government.

The Seven Steps were one of the last features to be removed during the demolition of District Six. Some of the flagstones were rescued and taken to a nearby church. They eventually ended up in the museum, which uses them as an integral part of its brand and logo. Today, the Seven Steps stand as a powerful symbol of the soul of the District Six community.

TAFELBERG DUTCH REFORMED CHURCH

Booming hymns from the green organ

Corner of Buitenkant and Commercial Streets
021-461-2682
Church services: Sunday at 9.30am

The building at the corner of Buitenkant and Commercial Streets doesn't look at all like a church. With its three gables, dormer and bay windows, it appears more like a grand colonial home than a religious building. Although the façade depicts a hodgepodge of styles, the interior is very fine indeed, with a magnificent organ as its centrepiece.

This complex dates from 1892 and includes the church building, Cornelia House, and the William Frederick School. Built for the Tafelberg Congregation (the architect was HJ Jones), it was inaugurated in 1893. The complex was declared a national monument in 1984.

Entering the church via a steep flight of steps between bay windows topped with pediments buttressed by Flemish scrolls, the visitor will discover a narrow foyer paved with ceramic tiles bearing biblical symbols from the Crucifixion and Judas's betrayal, a wooden spiral staircase that leads to a cast-iron gallery and a vast main hall with a high ceiling and simple, stained-glass windows of bright colour blocks. Its roof is supported by timber beams and trusses with trefoil motifs. The beautiful organ was installed in 1892 and has 1,164 pipes and a walnut case (the inner workings have been renewed).

The Tafelberg Dutch Reformed Church began life as a mission hall, the Cornelia Saal. It was part of a complex that included the adjoining building (for indigent women), the William Frederick School (closed in 1907) and an apartment on the building's second floor. The complex was given in trust to the church by Susanna Maria Hertzog in memory of her parents, William Frederik Hertzog and Susanna Cornelia Hertzog (née Hiddingh), and was built on the site of their old home. She stipulated that when a self-supporting congregation came into being, the complex would be transferred to the Dutch Reformed Church.

Dr JJ Kotzé, Dr Andrew Murray and Professor Marais conducted the inauguration ceremony on 27 January 1893. Cornelia Hertzog had the honour of unlocking the front door. Although services were held regularly from then on, the Tafelberg congregation was only founded in 1944, 47 years after Cornelia's death. The longest serving minister of the Tafelberg church was the Reverend JD Vorster (1935–1982), brother of former prime minister and state president John Vorster.

'WE ARE STILL HERE' MEMORIAL ⑤

A mosaic memorial to destitute children

Corner of Longmarket and Parade Streets

Behind the Cape Town Public Library lies a moving memorial to 7,000 children of all races who were sold as indentured labourers in the Cape Colony long after the abolition of slavery in 1833.

In 2006 Lance van Sittert of the UCT Department of Historical Studies discovered thousands of advertisements for orphaned and destitute children, which were published in the Cape Government Gazette between 1841 and 1921. The notices, often headed 'Destitute Child', listed the children's names, gender, race, age, where they were from and sometimes the circumstances that led to their abandonment. Children who were not claimed within six weeks of the notice would be apprenticed to 'fit and proper Persons' according to the law. Some of the children advertised were as young as a month old.

In 2011 funding from the Donald Gordon Creative Arts Award enabled the creation of a tribute to them. Local mosaic artist Lovell Friedman printed the adverts onto ceramic tiles, which are arranged to form the image of a child when viewed from a distance. Surrounding the adverts are drawings and writings by modern-day street children, also cast in enduring ceramic. The wall and the three square benches in front of it bear the trilingual Afrikaans, English and Xhosa title: 'Ons is nog hier – We are still here – Siselapha.'

Unfortunately, child labour and destitute children living on the streets remain an ongoing problem in South Africa. This memorial, while revealing some of the hidden brutality of the past, also serves as a reminder of the inadequate protection children receive in present-day society.

More Mosaics by Lovell Friedman

As part of a project by grassroots movement Rock Girl to create symbolic safe spaces in some of Cape Town's most challenged communities, Lovell Friedman has helped design 'Safe Spaces Benches' in Manenberg, Gugulethu and Khayelitsha. There's also one outside the Cape Town International Convention Centre.

The Mitchell's Plain Hospital features benches and colourful corridors lined with bright mosaics of hearts and hands by Lovell Friedman, who trained seven people from the local community to help her create them.

Friedman enlisted children from the Red Cross Children's Hospital Primary School in Rondebosch to help her make the tiles for the statue of Mother Courage that stands outside the new buildings.

Friedman's mosaics are also featured along the walkways of the bus station next to the Cape Town Stadium.

CITY HALL CARILLON

A WWI memorial rarely heard or seen

Cape Town City Hall, Darling Street
021-465-2029
By appointment only
Free entry

The Cape Town City Hall on the Grand Parade is a familiar landmark, but less well-known is that inside its 200-foot tower, just under the large clock (modelled on London's Big Ben), is a wonderful 39-bell carillon. It is the only playable carillon on the African continent. Although it is seldom rung these days, curious and intrepid visitors can arrange to see it by making an appointment with the city council.

Commissioned by the women of Cape Town as a monument to those who died in the First World War, it was proposed by the mayoress of Cape Town, Anna Thorne, just five days after the armistice. This was the first carillon conceived as a memorial to the Great War and many others followed in Allied countries. The bells are named after war zones in which South African troops fought.

The carillon was manufactured in 1923 by the English bell foundry Taylor & Co in Loughborough. The bells cost £3,300 (about £180,000 in today's money) and were transported free of charge by the Union Castle Mail Steamship Company. The carillon was inaugurated on 30 April 1925 on the occasion of HRH The Prince of Wales's visit. The first concerts were given by the Belgian carillonneur Anton Brees and the first song played was the hymn 'Oh God, Our Help in Ages Past '.

The carillon weighs 15.5 tons and is arranged in three layers, each with two rows of bells. It is played using a baton clavier (which looks like a cross between a loom and an organ) and there are hand batons and foot pedals connected to the bells by a complex system of cables. Using the claviers, a carillonneur can play any music from Beethoven to the Beatles. A room below the bells houses a practice clavier and a main clavier as well as a change ringing drum (which looks like a giant music box device) that can be used to play two different sequences. The tunes it plays are not identifiable.

The last master musician to play the Cape Town bells was the German carillon expert Ulrich Leykam in 2010.

Unfortunately, the bells and the steep narrow staircase you climb to reach them are somewhat dusty and neglected, so it's recommended that you bring a good head for heights and a torch if you visit.

A Carillon Played on the Release of Nelson Mandela

It was the sounds of the Cape Town carillon that the world heard on 11 February 1990 on the release of Nelson Mandela, who gave his first public speech as a free man from the balcony of the City Hall.

THE GENERAL POST OFFICE MURALS

Overlooked beautiful murals

Grand Central Building, corner of Darling Street and Plein Street
021 464 1770
Monday–Friday 8am–4.30pm (opens Wednesday at 8.30am)
Saturday 8am–1pm, Sunday Closed
Free entry

The General Post Office is often overlooked as eyes are drawn to the Old Mutual Building directly opposite. Even though they were built at the same time and opened within a few weeks of each other in

1940, the Old Mutual Building was hailed as the Art Deco masterpiece. It is, however, the inside of the Post Office that makes entry worthwhile.

Three artists were each commissioned to paint two murals, depicting historic scenes, in order to decorate the interior of the building. Enter the building from either Lower Plein Street or the pedestrian route next to the Trafalgar Flower Market, and you will meet a vibrant, eclectic mix of vendors, food stations and patrons there for general Post Office business. Look up towards the ceiling to find the six murals that are often ignored.

The first two are by J H Amshowitz. The first mural depicts the grand arrival of Jan van Riebeeck at Table Bay. In his second mural, the Castle of Good Hope is easily recognisable, but perhaps the lady less so. We owe much to Lady Anne Barnard, residing at the Cape between 1797–1802, a sort of 'First Lady' of Cape Town: her detailed diaries and water colour paintings offer a good understanding of life at the Cape in the early 19th century.

The second artist, G W Pilkington, composed the mural *Mail Boat Arriving at Table Bay Docks*, the most relevant of all the murals to the Post Office as the Union-Castle shipping line had a weekly mail service running between England and Cape Town. Along the same wall, the mural *The Landing of the 1820 Settlers at the Cape Colony* depicts the story of 4,000 settlers encouraged by the British government to migrate to South Africa, not only solving mass unemployment in England, but also helping increase the population of English-speakers at the Cape Colony.

It is artist Sydney Carter who brings alive the walls on either side of the Post Office area with two murals reflecting different heritage architectures: *Cape Dutch Architecture*, depicting distinctive gabled homes in country style settings, and *The Malay Quarter*, known today for the rows of brightly painted houses located in the Bo Kaap area.

Look for the postal stone built into an internal wall, located close to the entrance by the pedestrian street. It is surrounded by red tape to help you find it. Dating back to 1622, Captain Blythe has inscribed "here under look for letters". For more information about postal stones, see page 36.

LIGHTFOOT MEMORIAL FOUNTAIN

Commemorating a Cape Town hero

Trafalgar Place flower market
Corner of Trafalgar and Parliament Streets

Hidden away behind Adderley Street's flower sellers, barely noticed by pedestrians, lies the Lightfoot Memorial Fountain. The memorial is designed in the shape of a drinking fountain and was unveiled in 1907. Although somewhat worse for wear, it stands in honour of Archdeacon Thomas Lightfoot (1831–1904), a missionary who fought tirelessly for the poor of the city. He was a much-loved Capetonian and worked with all races and cultural groups, championing changes to discriminatory laws and tending to the sick.

Thomas Lightfoot was born and grew up in England, where he worked as a printer and newspaper reporter. In 1853 he was inspired to become a missionary and was ordained as a deacon in 1857. He arrived by ship in Cape Town a year later, aged 27. After taking charge of the new St Paul's Church in Bree Street, he devoted his life to mission work among the urban poor. He was known as a tireless doer and soon acquired the nickname 'The Southeaster'.

Lightfoot was one of the founders of free soup kitchens and night shelters for the homeless. Any money he received (including his paltry salary) went towards feeding the needy. He learnt High Dutch and Xhosa, translating parts of the English prayer book into High Dutch.

He opened a school for artisans and also worked among the convicts at Roeland Street Jail and the Breakwater Prison. During the great fever epidemic of 1867, he cared for the sick, and a ward in Somerset Hospital was named after him.

Lightfoot became a canon in 1870 and archdeacon of the Cape in 1885. His death on 12 November 1903, at the age of 73, was attributed to injuries sustained when he was blown over by the southeaster near to where his memorial now stands. To mark his passing, the bell of the new St George's Cathedral tolled for an hour. The town went into mourning and more than 4,000 people filed past his coffin in St Paul's. Three trains were needed to carry people to the cemetery for his interment. The Cape had never before seen such a funeral, not even in 1902 when Cecil John Rhodes's body passed through the streets on its way to Zimbabwe.

Made of red Verona marble, this three-metre fountain is a copy of the 14th-century original in the marketplace of Verona, Italy.

MULLERS OPTOMETRISTS

South Africa's first optometrists in a beautiful Art Déco building

104 Longmarket Street
Monday–Friday 8am–5pm, Saturday 9am–1pm

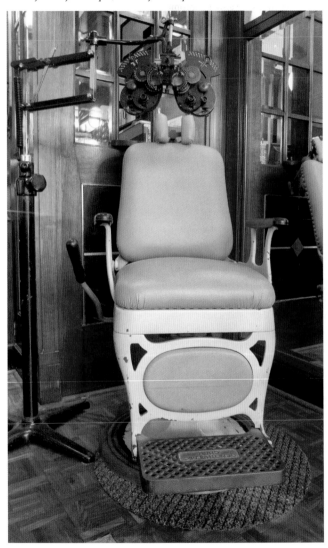

Tucked away on the quiet corner of Longmarket and Parliament Streets stands an iconic black-and-white Art Deco building, home to South Africa's first optometry practice. Mullers has been run by the same family since 22-year-old Joseph Muller arrived from Germany in 1890 and became Cape Town's first qualified optician. He was followed by two of his five sons and three of his grandsons. His great-grandson, Peter Muller, is now also an optometrist and partner in the business.

Joseph Muller initially combined his optometry practice with watch-making and jewellery. The business moved from an adjacent building to the current premises in 1920. The black-slate and chrome shopfront was designed by Frank Spears, a multi-talented British painter, broadcaster and boat designer, who was a household name in Cape Town's cultural circles at the time. Trained as a designer of shopfronts, Spears's work once adorned the façades of many city buildings, of which Mullers is probably the finest example still existing.

The shop's interior remains almost as it was a century ago, while accommodating an informal museum of the history of eye care in Cape Town. Photographs, historic optometric equipment, an early examining chair, an old crank telephone and antique furniture are all on display, along with one of Cape Town's oldest working elevators. Clocks from Joseph Muller's original watchmaking business are still in use.

Joseph Muller's name was the 79th entry in the register of the British Optical Association, founded in 1895 as the first professional body for opthalmic opticians in the world. His diploma, signed by the association's first president and secretary, is on display. Mullers' carefully preserved records chronicle the evolution of eye care in South Africa as well as their many distinguished patients, including Sir Joseph Milner, governor of the Cape Colony until 1899, and Sir Walter Heley-Hutchinson, Governor-General of Natal until 1901, along with numerous cabinet ministers and politicians.

Today there are six Mullers branches in Cape Town.

Thanks to its proximity to parliament, Mullers has been witness to numerous milestones in South Africa's history, from the colonial era to the release of Mandela. Peter Muller's great-uncle had to defend the shop against anti-German mobs during World War I and the building is still pockmarked by rubber bullets shot at protesters during the 70s and 80s.

WOODEN COBBLES

Original wooden cobbles dating back more than 150 years

Corner of Adderley and Spin Streets, outside the Groote Kerk

When a bicycle lane was constructed on Adderley Street, the most significant nod to heritage was the relaying of a small patch of wooden cobbles that were found under the pavement.

A construction crew upgrading the city's pedestrian and cycle lanes in August 2010 uncovered the closely fitted wooden setts (cobbles) while they were digging up the road surface. The City of Cape Town and Heritage Western Cape agreed to preserve a section of the road near the Groote Kerk to allow Capetonians and visitors to view a part of the street dating to 1856.

The city employed a team of specialists to restore a 10-metre-long by one-metre-wide section of the cobbles. A wooden tray was made to accommodate the setts, which were removed by hand and placed on the tray in their original positions. The tray was then stored under cover.

As the roadwork neared completion, a sand bed was laid and the cobbles were relaid in the footway close to the spot from where they were removed. A bitumen-and-sand mixture was swept into the joints to seal them and a clear resin was applied to the wooden cobbles for their protection.

Cape Town's roads were originally dirt and would later have been paved with packed rock. Later, these rocks were sealed with poured bitumen and eventually covered with asphalt. Wooden setts weren't common in Cape Town and were usually laid in a bid to quieten the noise caused by horse's hooves and steel cart wheels on the packed rock.

The fact that these setts were found outside the Groote Kerk indicates that they were laid for noise abatement. Adderley Street was the hub of Cape Town and would have been bustling with horse-drawn carriages, carts and cabs.

It is not clear exactly what wood was used, but it is thought to have been jarrah or have come from shipwrecks. Norwegian pine was also frequently used for wooden cobbles in cities in northern Europe and North America.

THE VAULT OF OLOF BERGH

The resting place of one of Cape Town's most successful scoundrels

The Groote Kerk
Parliament Street
Monday–Friday 10am–2pm
Free entry

As the oldest church in South Africa, the Groote Kerk is one of the best-known landmarks in Cape Town. Visitors to the church can scarcely fail to notice the great church organ – the largest in the country – and the magnificent, carved pulpit, the work of sculptor Anton Anreith. Yet no casual visitor would be likely to notice a small piece of Batavian soapstone paving near the entrance, which bears a simple inscription: 'O. Bergh 3'.

About 200 prominent Capetonians were buried in vaults beneath the church's floor, including eight governors. Simon van der Stel, the first governor of the Cape, is beneath the pulpit, and the 'pickled baron' (see page 67) is also here, although his gravestone is mounted on the wall outside. Apparently the practice of burying wealthy worshippers under churches, where they were left to decompose, led to the phrase 'stinking rich'. And Olof Bergh, whose grave is marked by the stone, most certainly was.

Bergh arrived at the Cape in 1676, a keen young sergeant in the Dutch East India Company (VOC). Van der Stel sent him on many missions, including salvaging the cargo of an English ship, *Joanna*, which sank near Gansbaai in 1682.

In 1686, when the Portuguese ship, *Nossa Senhora de los Milagros*, carrying gifts to the kings of England, France and Portugal from the King of Siam, was wrecked at Cape Agulhas, Van der Stel made Bergh part of that salvage team too. But when the party returned to Cape Town, they handed only a few pieces of soiled treasure over to the council. Rumours abounded, and after one of the salvagers sold several valuable items to a resident, company officials searched Bergh's garden and dug up a cache of loot.

Bergh admitted to his part in the theft, but unwisely implicated Van der Stel in the affair, saying the governor knew about it and had told him to keep quiet. Bergh was imprisoned on Robben Island until the VOC offered him a job in Ceylon. In 1695 he returned to the Cape as a captain. He was pardoned for his crimes and appointed commander of the garrison.

When Bergh died, aged 80, he was one of the wealthiest men in the Cape and a sizeable landowner – an uncanny achievement on a company official's salary! Bergh even bought Constantia from Van der Stel's estate. Like his former master, he died there and was buried just a few feet away in the same church.

POSTAL STONES

A fantastic and smart way to send a letter back home in the 17th century ...

Slave Lodge
Corner of Adderley and Wale Streets
021 467 7229
iziko.org.za/museums/slave-lodge
Opening times: check website for details

Inside the Slave Lodge, the second oldest building in Cape Town, six stones, labelled "postal stones", are located in a room just off the courtyard and are easily missed while walking through this museum.

Five of these postal stones date back to the early 17th century: a journey from Europe to the Cape could take several months and sailors would relish the opportunity to stop and replenish ship supplies for the next leg of their journey to the East. They would mostly collect fresh water, and trade with the local Khoi and San, some five decades prior to any form of European settlement. The concept of the postal stone was clever – it was a mariner's device for expediating letters back home. Sailors would leave their letters under a postal stone, and the returning ships from the East, also looking to stock-up on supplies, would retrieve the letters and take the messages home.

Typically, a postal stone would be engraved with the name of ship, the captain, and the dates of arrival and departure. Sometimes a postal stone was re-used, and in some cases, a second inscription can be seen.

Despite numerous French ships passing through the Cape, only one postal stone with a French inscription has ever been found, inscribed with "David Digaed arrived from Dieppe, 8th day of February 1640". This stone had already been used by the Dutch, as on the reverse you can read the Dutch inscription from 1633.

The story of the postal stones holds a special place in our heritage landscape. Except for one found in Mossel Bay (with Portuguese inscriptions), which is the oldest one dating to 1505, they have all been found in the vicinity of Cape Town, usually having been stumbled upon accidentally during roadworks or other general development in Cape Town. Fortunately for us, the builders have taken care to hand them over to the appropriate authorities.

An additional postal stone

While viewing the Post Office Murals close by (see p. 26), seek out the postal stone built into the inside wall in the corner of the Post Office, located on the pedestrian side entrance, next to the exit towards the underground walkway. It has been surrounded by red tape to make it easier to find. Dated 1622, Captain Blythe has inscribed "here under look for letters". The additional date 1629 inscribed at the bottom, reflects the re-use of the stone.

THE COAT OF ARMS OF THE TOWN HOUSE

The first coat of arms in South Africa

Greenmarket Square

Greenmarket Square is a visual feast of heritage buildings and market vendors, so it is easy to miss the very first coat of arms ever used in South Africa. Standing in front of The Old Town House, look up and notice a red shield containing three gold circles, sitting on an anchor – it was presented in 1804.

During the early 19th century, the Cape Colony was transitioning through some interesting politics. The original Dutch Republic had come to an end, and from 1803–1806 the revolutionary Batavian Republic, which had replaced it in the Netherlands, also took control of the Cape. The new Commissioner-General, Jacob De Mist, was sent to the Cape to establish new regulations and install Dutch officials. He was a man who valued the importance of tradition and heraldry and, on 3 July 1804, he presented the coat of arms in grand ceremonial style, attended by dignitaries who enjoyed trumpets, speeches and a splendid banquet.

The anchor represents Good Hope and the wish for the future wealth and prosperity of the settlement. It is protected by a red shield bearing three gold rings, the coat of arms belonging to the van Riebeeck family (at this time, Jan van Riebeeck was considered to be the founding father of the settlement). The fact that Jan van Riebeeck had a family crest is a testament to his family's legacy.

By contrast, nine years earlier, the Batavian government in the Netherlands itself had abolished all coats of arms, declaring them to be contrary to equality, making it somewhat remarkable that it was Batavian representatives who introduced them into a place where they had never existed.

The Old Town House is one of our best examples of 18th-century architecture, and it makes sense that this building was selected to install the first coat of arms since it represents the beginning of local government in South Africa. In 1657, when the Dutch East India Company was looking to reduce expenses, it offered select employees 'free land' and hence created the free burgher (free citizens), marking the beginning of permanent settlement at the Cape. Soon after, there was a need for a town council and the Town House became the local government administration building for a century, until the new City Hall on Grand Parade was completed in 1905.

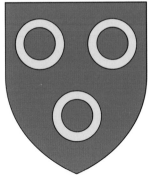

It is interesting how the next coat of arms for the Cape Colony still incorporated the three gold rings into the more elaborate design which can be seen on the City Hall today.

THE SLAVE CHURCH MUSEUM

South Africa's oldest mission church

40 Long Street
Monday–Friday 9am–4pm
Free entry

Although it's one of Long Street's oldest and most beautiful buildings, the guest book reveals that the Slave Church Museum is not visited very frequently. Completed in 1802, it's the oldest mission church in South Africa and the third oldest church of any denomination still in its original form – Cape Town's first church, the Groote Kerk, was almost entirely rebuilt in 1841.

The South African Missionary Institution (Sendingsgestig) was founded in 1799 by four missionaries – two Dutch and two English – who were sent by the London Missionary Society to promote mission work at the Cape. The Sendingsgestig's main purpose was not to conduct religious services, but rather to provide literacy training and Bible classes to the 'heathen' of Cape Town, particularly the slaves, hence it became known as the 'Slave Church'.

The church was built by the master mason Johan Gottfried Mocke and master carpenter Joseph van Schalkover, assisted by slaves and free black people. It was the first South African church to be built in the form of a basilica with a curved apse. The exterior features four Corinthian pilasters, a dentilled cornice, a Cape gable with four urns and front steps made of Robben Island slate. It also has the only remaining example of a lime-concrete roof, which was annually waterproofed with whale oil.

Inside, it is furnished with oak pews, an organ and a neo-classical pulpit with two staircases. Two elegant teak columns (made from a single ship's mast) support the main gallery, constructed of yellowwood and teak. The front porch was known as a wind-lobby, as the three doors could be opened or closed depending on the wind's direction.

In the 50s and 60s, thanks to urban racial segregation, most of the congregation was re-settled in the Cape Flats and the building became dilapidated. When it was sold in 1971, it was in danger of being demolished and by 1977 part of its northern wall had collapsed. Fortunately, in 1978 the provincial authorities decided to restore it. The renovation team was aided by an 1830s drawing of the original façade.

NEARBY
Cape Town's Oldest Elevator

Next door, in the foyer of the Grand Daddy Hotel, which opened in 1895 as the Hotel Metropole, is what is claimed to be the city's oldest operational elevator. Take a ride in it to the top floor, climb the stairs to the roof and you'll find Cape Town's only rooftop trailer park, where you can stay overnight in one of the Airstream trailers, each individually decorated by local artists.

THE HERITAGE VINE

Probably the oldest wine-producing vine in the southern hemisphere

Corner of Bree and Shortmarket Streets
Courtyard accessible via Heritage Square Hotel
Free entry

In a courtyard surrounded by historic townhouses grows an ancient vine that still produces a few litres of wine each year. Estimated to have been planted in 1771, it's likely that this is not only the oldest vine in South Africa, but also the oldest wine-producing vine in the southern hemisphere.

Wine-making in the Cape dates back to the first days of the Dutch settlement. Scurvy, caused by Vitamin C deficiency, was the scourge of sailors of the day. It was the main reason Jan van Riebeeck was sent to establish a refreshment station at the Cape in 1652. Commander van Riebeeck had been an assistant surgeon in Batavia and believed (incorrectly) that wine could cure scurvy. Naturally, planting vines was among his first actions on arrival. Seven years later, on 2 February 1659, he wrote in his diary, "Today, praise be to God, wine was made for the first time from Cape grapes."

The vines of The Company Gardens did not last long before wine-making moved first to Constantia then Franschhoek, Paarl and Stellenbosch. However, it remained common for the burghers of Cape Town to plant vines in their gardens and make their own wine. This was probably the case with the vine at Heritage Square. The townhouses were built in 1771 and in a journal dated 1785 the first landlord wrote, "Drinking wine under the grape tree." In 2008 (223 years later) the vine again produced 15 litres of excellent wine, made on the premises and bottled with the label 'Heritage 1771'.

That the vine exists at all is something of a miracle. In the mid-1800s, European vineyards were obliterated by the Phylloxera aphid in The Great French Wine Blight. Phylloxera spread to the Cape in 1866, causing widespread devastation. Probably owing to its isolation, the Heritage vine escaped the blight, making it one of the few remaining original French vinifera rootstock surviving today.

Then, in the 1960s, the townhouses were threatened with demolition in order to build a multi-storey car park. For over a decade, the square was left abandoned and the vine survived untended, fed only by rainwater. Luckily, the car park project fell through and the Cape Town Heritage Trust, formed in 1987, undertook to renovate the square.

The Heritage vine is so old that it is difficult to accurately identify the variety. Initial research suggested it was a Crouchen Blanc, one of the first varieties to arrive in the Cape from the western Pyrenees. However, when winemaker and viticulturist Jean Vincent Rindon sent cuttings to the French National Institute for Agricultural Research, he was told the vine is probably a Gros Chenin, better known as Chenin Blanc.

HISTORIC TRAM TRACKS

The remainder of an almost forgotten transport network

St Andrews Square
Corner of Somerset Road and Buitengracht Street

In a quiet square in the middle of one of Cape Town's busiest traffic intersections, a preserved section of tram tracks was discovered during the construction of the Prestwich Memorial in 2007. The tracks are the

remainder of an almost forgotten city transport network.

Cape Town's first horse-drawn trams started running in 1863 from Adderley Street along this part of Somerset Road to Green Point. In 1896 they were converted to electric and on 9 November 1901 the tramline was extended along Sea Point to Camps Bay. A second line from Cape Town to Camps Bay over Kloof Nek opened exactly a year later.

Both lines were considerable feats of engineering as the trams had to safely negotiate steep gradients and sharp curves – but passengers could now ride a circular route around the mountain.

The 12-mile round trip took just over 40 minutes and the tram ride was described in an old Cape Town guide as being "without doubt the most beautiful in the world." The trams were advertised overseas as a major tourist attraction and members of the British Royal Family took the trip to Camps Bay and back.

However, the real objective of the new tramway was to open up Camps Bay to sell land for development. Unfortunately, the depression following the Second Anglo-Boer War foiled these plans. In 1902 about 27,000 people left Cape Town. Camps Bay land prices remained low and the trams were less profitable than hoped for.

The last Camps Bay tram ran on 16 February 1930. Usable parts were repurposed to build the new Cape Town trolleybuses, referred to by locals as 'trackless trams'. These ran until 1939.

The original Camps Bay Tramway power station still stands and is now the Theatre on the Bay.

The Old Tram Route

Passengers could enjoy an uninterrupted journey from the city to Camps Bay and back. Starting in central Adderley Street, the trams proceeded up Wale Street and Buitengracht to the corner of Burnside Road. Here the line joined the track up Kloof Nek Road and over the Nek. Descending into Camps Bay, the terminus was in front of the Rotunda Hotel in Victoria Road (now the five-star Bay Hotel). Continuing back to Cape Town via Sea Point took you along Kloof Road, which joined the track on Main Road Sea Point at the junction of Regent Road. Trams then proceeded down Somerset Road and Waterkant, turning briefly into Long Street and down Strand Street back to Adderley.

PRESTWICH MEMORIAL

The bones of Cape Town's forgotten dead

Corner of Buitengracht Street and Somerset Road
021-418-0073
Monday–Friday 7am–5pm, Saturday–Sunday 8am–1pm

The Prestwich Memorial is a curious-looking building with a façade of Robben Island slate set in a garden beside St Andrew's Square. It houses an ossuary and a number of interpretive displays, including a copy of the 360-degree panorama of Table Bay painted by Robert Gordon in 1778.

This modern ossuary marks the final resting place of more than 2,500 people. The skeletons were exhumed from a building site at the corner of Prestwich and Albert Streets. The unmarked graves are thought to include everyone from servants, slaves and washerwomen to sailors and those executed by the colonial government between the second half of the 18th century and the late 19th century. The remains reveal a diversity of cultural, racial and religious origins: a microcosm of the multi-cultural Cape.

In colonial Cape Town, many people were denied access to church graveyards and were buried in unmarked graves in unofficial cemeteries. The Prestwich Memorial pays tribute to these forgotten citizens and to the legacy of slavery in the city. The remains are kept in boxes on shelves in the ossuary (many are simply numbered, as no identities were recorded).

The Green Point and De Waterkant areas have long been places of class and racial conflict. During the early colonial period, this zone was used as a burial ground for the 'unwanted'. In the 1820s, the area was sub-divided and plots were sold, making it part of the urban core of the growing city. In the 1960s, black and coloured citizens were forcibly removed to the Cape Flats.

Then in 2003, building activity in the area uncovered human bones and, as required by the South African Heritage Resources Agency Act, construction was halted. Archaeologists from the University of Cape Town were contracted to investigate.

Exhumation of the human remains began, even though a public consultation process had not yet been finalised. This led to further conflict among academics, civil-society groups, developers and government officials. Eventually, a solution was agreed upon by most parties. The City of Cape Town approved the funding and construction of an ossuary on a nearby site. The Prestwich Memorial and Visitors Centre was built to serve as a place of remembrance, commemorating all the unnamed people who helped build the Mother City.

AUWAL MOSQUE

South Africa's first and oldest mosque

34 Dorp Street
Visitors are welcome but should wear trousers or skirts, cover their heads and remove their shoes
Daily 6am–8pm, but avoid entering during prayers
Prayer times: 1pm, 4pm, 6.15pm and 7.30pm (prayers last 15–30 minutes)

The small neighbourhood of Bo-Kaap is best known for its colourful houses, but within its confines are no less than 10 mosques. Although it is by no means the most prominent of the Bo-Kaap's mosques, the Auwal (or Owal) Mosque, sandwiched tightly between the terraced houses on Dorp Street, is certainly the most important.

Oral tradition places it as the first formal Islamic mosque in South Africa. Although Islam was not forbidden during the Dutch rule of the Cape, the Dutch East India Company (VOC) did not allow any places of worship to be built other than Dutch Reformed Churches, so Muslims had to perform religious services outdoors or in their imam's homes.

The exact origins of the mosque are shrouded in mystery. The mosque itself bears a plaque saying it was established in 1794, but it's unlikely that this would have been permitted before the first British occupation of the Cape in 1795. One version of the mosque's history says the property was purchased in 1794 by a vryezwarten (freed black slave), Coridan van Ceylon. He passed it to his son-in-law, Achmat van Bengalen, who made it available for use as a mosque in 1798. Other sources claim the property was donated by a woman, Saartjie van de Kaap, who is said to have been either the imam's wife or the granddaughter of Coridan van Ceylon. But her ownership of the property only dates back to 1809. Still others say that the British administration gave permission for the building, originally a warehouse, to be converted into a mosque in 1797.

However, all sources agree that the mosque's first imam was Abdullah ibn Kadi Abd al-Salam, also known as Tuan Guru. A prince of Tidore, he was banished by the VOC to the Cape in 1780 and imprisoned on Robben Island for twelve years, where he is said to have written several copies of the Quran from memory. Sadly, one of these handwritten copies went missing from the Auwal Mosque in 2008.

When Tuan Guru died in 1807, a dispute arose as to who should be his successor, and a portion of the congregation split off to form the Palm Tree Mosque on Long Street. Achmat van Bengalen eventually became imam of the Auwal Mosque in 1822, but died a year later aged 93. In 1930 part of the mosque collapsed and major alterations followed, including the addition of the prayer minaret. The mosque was again renovated and expanded in 1986 and only two of the original walls now remain.

DUTCH MANOR ANTIQUE HOTEL ⑲

The elegance of old Cape Town

158 Buitengracht Street
021-422-4767
info@dutchmanor.co.za

The Dutch Manor is a graceful house on the edge of the colourful suburb of Bo-Kaap on the slopes of Signal Hill. Today, it serves as an antique hotel, restored to showcase the elegance of 19th-century Cape Town.

The double-storeyed, three-bay building has a high stoep with the front door opening onto what is virtually the second floor. The door features an original fanlight, with slightly curved top and a shaped transom. The upper storey has two, tall sash windows with fixed upper lights and curved tops. There are fluted pilasters near the corners, while the central portion of the façade projects slightly.

The Dutch Manor stands on an erf granted in 1811 by the 'Raad der Gemeente' to a trader named Johannes Joachim Theron. The house dates from that time (probably 1812). As Theron owned the property until 1824, he was most likely also the builder. Later that century it served as the Nova Scotia Hotel and went on to see life as a home for a family of 17, a lawyers' office and even a brothel. The building was restored by architect Gawie Fagan in 1990 and proclaimed a national monument the following year.

The house is decorated with typical town furniture of the period, crafted at the Cape, some of it in the Bo-Kaap. From the moment you step inside, you are transported back to colonial times. There's a mahogany reception desk (dated 6 May 1852) and a red carpet displaying the logo of Jan van Riebeeck, first commander of the Cape.

The manor has high ceilings and creaky floors, while thick walls and heavily brocaded drapes mute the noise of traffic. There's fine silverware, delicate Delft-style ceramics and bookshelves filled with well-thumbed classics. It boasts a number of fine furniture pieces, from yellowwood and stinkwood half-moon tables to a dinner table that dates back to 1710. The upstairs lounge has two armchairs from the old Union Parliament, a calf-leather lounge suite and a heavily embossed stinkwood armoire. There are gilded mirrors, embossed lamps and large bunches of flowers spilling from vases.

The bedrooms have wooden armoires, jonkmanskaste and four-poster beds from various periods (including a rare babbeljoentjie bed draped in French lace), as well as handcrafted kists and riempie couches.

MANNENBERG MEMORIAL

Run a stick along the metal pipes to hear the famous freedom tune Mannenberg

21 Bloem Street

Tucked away on the wall of 21 Bloem Street, close to Long Street, lies a unique interactive memorial that combines history, music,

interactive art, and politics. Resembling a type of geyser, pedestrians barely notice it – it is in fact a simple but ingenious piece of remembrance art.

Commissioned in 2006 by the *Sunday Times* newspaper for their centenary celebrations, the Mannenberg memorial was a unique collaboration of skills between electrical engineer Mark O'Donovan and performing artist Francois Venter.

Seven metal pipes were moulded, welded and mounted on to the wall of the original music studio, where the freedom song *Mannenberg* was recorded in June 1974. The concept is the following: run a stick along these seven metal pipes and you will hear the opening notes to the famous freedom tune *Mannenberg*.

Abdullah Ibrahim (born 1934) was a leading musician of Cape Jazz and Marabi. In June 1974 he was experimenting with tunes with his fellow musicians when the song *Mannenberg* was produced at this spot. This freedom song was created against the backdrop of harsh apartheid politics and forced removals, where non-white citizens were evicted from their homes in the city and relocated to the outer suburbs.

Cape Jazz is a sub-genre of jazz performed in South Africa, whilst Marabi is a type of piano-style music, initially created underground as much of the content was against the national politics at the time. Ibrahim's music reflects influences from his childhood and the effects of apartheid politics.

Typical music venues where it was played were shebeens (township style bars) – the music provided a much-needed daily opportunity for enjoyment and hope for the future.

The township Manenberg (after which the song was named with a change in spelling), was established in 1966 at the height of the Group Areas Act. Located around 20 km outside the city, Manenberg was one of multiple non-white suburbs created by the National Party, and it suffered from over-crowding, minimal commercial opportunities and high unemployment. In addition, the location meant that these newly displaced residents now had to endure long journeys to work and school.

The song had a huge impact in the community and was played regularly at political rallies.

It is recommended that you google the Manneberg tune and listen to it before visiting the memorial. Or better still, listen to the tune on your device while running a stick along the pipes.

CENTRE FOR THE BOOK

Edwardian home of reading

62 Queen Victoria Street
021-423-2669
cbreception@nlsa.ac.za
Monday–Friday 8am–4pm and Saturday 8am–1pm, closed on Sunday

First opened in 1913 as headquarters of the short-lived University of Good Hope, the Centre for the Book is a grand Edwardian building that was declared a national monument in 1990. More recently it has become an annexe of the National Library of South Africa. The Centre for the Book has a home in this structure on the periphery of the Company's Garden. Visit it to view the gracious architecture and to discover local literary talent.

The building has a fine exterior of intricately carved sandstone, a roof of green faïence Spanish tiles and a copper-coated dome crowned by a teak cupola. The vast Ceremonial Hall is half-moon in shape with pilasters, a skylight and a large chandelier. The hall's upper shelves house collections belonging to the National Library, while the lower shelves showcase works by contemporary South African authors.

The centre is an outreach arm of the National Library of South Africa. Its main mission is to promote a culture of reading, writing and publishing in local languages through easy access to books for all. It gathers and distributes information, provides advice and guidance on matters relating to books, publishing, creative writing and literacy. To this end it produces brochures, pamphlets, booklets and newsletters, many of which are on display. It also facilitates the reprinting of books considered to be classics of South Africa's indigenous languages.

Along with developing programmes and activities that support and nurture budding authors, the centre occasionally conducts workshops on editing, manuscript development and book marketing in order to empower young writers. It has converted one of its studios into a Children's Reading Centre in partnership with the Ukuhamba Nabatwana Trust, which provides opportunities for children up to the age of seven to read books for pleasure, write their own stories, watch puppet shows and be entertained by storytellers. The centre also donates books and posters to schools, libraries, art centres and organisations involved in reading promotion. To date, more than 40,000 children, mostly in rural areas, have received eight books each. In addition, the centre's efforts to introduce children to books at an early age has seen the development of a children's library in the rural town of Mount Ayliff in the Eastern Cape. Through these laudable efforts, the grand old Edwardian lady of Queen Victoria Street is giving back to young South Africa.

THE PUMP TREE

22

An old pump embedded in a tree stump

The Company's Garden, Queen Victoria Street
7am–8.30pm in summer and 7am–7pm in winter
Free entry

Visitors may come across the stone well in the middle of the lower section of the Company's Garden. Those with sharp eyes will notice the pump handle and spout protruding from the stump of an oak tree a short distance away.

The remains of the hand pump are dated 1842 and the well it adjoins was built at the same time. The old oak was felled by a storm in 2015, but the city restored its stump, with the embedded hand pump, for posterity.

The pump was connected to the well by an underground pipe. Looking down into the well it's possible to see a small section of the original slate covering juts out over the top of the red brick.

Constructed from imported bricks, the well had a depth of 2.7m (9 feet). The reason the well is relatively shallow is that it was built like a sump. At regular intervals down the shaft are wooden layers, on top of which rest layers of brick and shale. This allowed ground water to filter into the well.

Before 1850 there were a number of wells in the Garden, but when a proper water service was provided, they were abandoned and filled in.

The Oldest Tree in the Garden

The saffron pear tree in the Company's Garden is probably the oldest cultivated tree in South Africa. It was brought from Holland in Van Riebeeck's time, about 350 years ago.

One of the original varieties of pear, *Pyrus communis*, it is known as the common or saffron pear and bears small fruit. Traditionally, the leaves were used to dye wool a distinctive saffron yellow and the fruit was used in pickles and preserves.

The tree's original trunk collapsed many years ago. What remains are four sprouts that emerged from the roots. The ancient branches are held up by metal crutches and cables and protected by a fence. In August 2013, cuttings were taken to preserve the tree's genetic material. Should the original tree die, a clone could be planted in its place.

LIBERMAN DOORS

23

A remarkable treasure of Jewish history

Courtyard of the National Gallery
Government Avenue, Company Gardens
021 481 3970
iziko.org.za/museums/south-african-national-gallery
Open seven days a week: check website for details

Within the courtyard of the National Gallery, the Liberman Doors are a little-known but remarkable treasure of Jewish history, carved exquisitely in wood.

Born in Poland and raised in England, Hyman Liberman (1853–1923) arrived in Cape Town aged 20. A successful businessman, he became the first Jewish Mayor in Cape Town, serving three terms (1904–1907). He was involved with the grand openings of the City Hall and the Great Synagogue (1905), and upon his death, bequeathed his wealth to a range of multi-cultural charities, with 10,000 pounds being set aside for a piece of public art to be enjoyed by everyone, namely the Liberman doors.

Herbert Meyerowitz (1900–1945), a man of similar heritage to Liberman, was commissioned to complete the doors, a task that took him four years. Born in St Petersburg (Russia), he arrived in South Africa in 1925 where he established a studio, before becoming the first lecturer in wood carving at the Michaelis School of Fine Art. In preparation, Meyerowitz did numerous sketches and designs in plaster before carving the doors. Burmese teak was selected for its durability in tropical climates, high resistance to insects and because it transitions to a dark golden sheen during aging.

When you first see the doors, it is immediately striking how Meyerowitz had the extraordinary ability to fill every square inch with intricate details, with multiple stories in one carving.

Hebrew migrations from around the world begin at the base on both sides, moving upwards until they arrive in the land of peace of prosperity (South Africa) on the lintel. Immigrants can be seen boarding ships, which still resonates with the local community today, the majority having either Russian or Lithuanian heritage. The pogroms of Russia and Eastern Europe precipitated a mass exodus of Jews, and news of gold discovery on the Witswaterand in 1886 made the ships sailing for Cape Town an attractive option.

On the lintel, the gabled houses are representative of the Cape Dutch architecture prevalent at the time. On the right, a man wears a hat and cloak pushing a barrow. These gentlemen were affectionately known as *smous* (pedlars): they would purchase stock from merchants in Cape Town then travel throughout the interior, selling their wares door to door. Every time you look at the doors you notice something different.

NETSUKE MINIATURE CARVINGS ㉔

One of the world's finest collections of Japanese miniature art

South African Jewish Museum
88 Hatfield Street
Sunday–Thursday 10am–5pm; Friday 10am–2pm; closed Saturdays and Jewish holidays
Identification required

Lying in the basement of the South African Jewish Museum is one of the largest and finest collections of Japanese miniature art in the world.

In a small room lined with wooden cabinets, more than 200 carvings and ornamental sword fittings are displayed, each in separate compartments, like a giant printer's tray. Fashioned from wood, ivory, staghorn and bone, the carvings are astonishingly intricate and lifelike. Visitors can spend hours poring over them – magnifying glasses and descriptive pamphlets are provided.

About half the exhibit is composed of *netsuke* – miniature ceremonial carvings worn by wealthy merchants during the time of the Samurai. The development of netsuke can be traced back to the Seclusion (Sakoku) Edict of 1635. Concerned with the burgeoning wealth of the merchants, the Shogun forbade all classes other than samurai from flaunting their wealth on pain of death.

However, utilitarian objects were exempt from these laws. As kimonos didn't have pockets, Japanese men wore small boxes (*inro*) or pouches (*obi*) hung from their sashes by a cord attached with a bobble. These bobbles were netsuke, which became one of the few ways the merchant classes could display their status. The accessories quickly evolved into miniature works of art.

Isaac Kaplan, one of the founders of the South African Jewish Museum, was introduced to Japanese *okimono* (ornamental art) by a friend who visited Japan in the 1930s. Kaplan developed a lifelong passion for Japanese miniature art, particularly *netsuke* and sword fittings, collecting a total of 613 Japanese carvings through London trading houses and auctions, of which the best are on display here. Their subjects are drawn from every facet of Japanese life: history, mythology, religion and popular humour. From a deer howling at the moon to a tea kettle becoming a badger, the objects are both breathtakingly beautiful and intriguing. For example, one *netsuke* (an ivory pine cone) opens to reveal, on one side, an old couple sweeping pine needles and on the other, a 1000-year old turtle (*minogame*) and a crane beneath a pine tree. All this in a carving just four centimetres high.

Interestingly, Kaplan never visited Japan himself. He spent hours every evening studying Japanese art, history, legend and culture to enhance his insight into the pieces in his collection. He even taught himself to read and write the Japanese of the Samurai period. But Kaplan reasoned that since his passion was for the bygone world of 17th- and 18th-century Japan, he would not want to see the changes that had taken place there since.

Relics of Cape Town's Robinson Crusoe

Mountain Club of South Africa
97 Hatfield Street
Monday–Friday 10am–2pm
Free entry

In 1892 a member of the Mountain Club came upon a small cave near the top of Fountain Ravine on Table Mountain. Inside the cave were relics thought to have been left behind by Joshua Penny, a deserter who had hidden on the mountain a hundred years before. When the Mountain Club of South Africa obtained a rare copy of Penny's memoirs in 1957, they mounted an expedition to retrieve the objects and they are now housed in the club's headquarters in Gardens. Two small, glass-fronted cases contain a variety of items, including pieces of fabric and buttons, clay pipes, flint and steels, charred antelope and dassie bones, along with the remains of the Guernsey coat Penny was wearing when he escaped.

The story of Joshua Penny is somewhat ironic. As an American seaman who was press-ganged into the British Navy, Penny hated the English and was desperate to escape. When HMS *Sceptre*, on which he was serving, docked in Cape Town in mid October 1799, Penny, who had been feigning sickness for several months after a fight with the ship's bully, saw an opportunity. On his way to the naval hospital, the patient treated his two-man escort to a bottle at a local tavern, then promptly ran off and hid on Table Mountain.

For 14 months, the 26-year-old lived alone on the mountain, purportedly surviving on a diet of antelope, dassie meat and beer made from wild honey, while waiting for the *Sceptre* to sail out of the bay. Penny finally returned to the harbour and saw just one ship left in it. He was told by its Danish captain that the *Sceptre* had been wrecked at Woodstock Beach in a storm on 5 November 1799, only a couple of weeks after he'd made his getaway. Most of the crew had died and it was highly unlikely that the survivors would have come looking for him.

Penny left Cape Town on the Danish ship and eventually managed to return to New York, where he published his memoirs in 1815. Needless as his long concealment turned out to be, he appears to have enjoyed his months on the mountain. He wrote that, "every night [I] could sing my song with as much pleasure as at any period of my life. In fine, I never enjoyed life better than while I lived among the ferocious animals of Table Mountain; because I had secured myself against the more savage English."

THE QUAGGA FOAL

A lonely foal sparks the resurrection of an extinct zebra

South African Museum
25 Queen Victoria Street
Daily 10am–5pm

Tucked away in a gloomy room of the South African Museum is a tiny quagga foal – one of only 23 remaining specimens of an extinct type of zebra once plentiful in southern Africa. If you don't know she's there, you'll probably miss her, as her case is kept completely darkened – a switch must be pressed to illuminate her for just a few seconds. It is thanks to this foal, and to an extraordinary natural historian named Reinhold Rau, that her kind may once again wander the dusty plains of the Karoo.

When colonists arrived in the Cape, quaggas were ruthlessly hunted and many were sent to European zoos. However, because the term 'quagga' was used indiscriminately to refer to all zebras, its extinction in the wild in 1878 passed unnoticed. When a quagga mare at Amsterdam Zoo died on 12 August 1883, nobody realised she was the very last of her kind. Indeed, it was only three years later that quagga hunting was banned in the Cape.

When Rau was tasked with remounting the South African Museum's shabby quagga foal in 1969, he discovered that there was still flesh attached to the pelt. Rau kept the tissue and notified the scientific community. But it was only much later, in 1983, that Russell Higuchi from the University of California requested tissue samples for DNA testing.

The quagga became the first extinct animal to have its DNA studied. The results were astonishing: instead of being a distinct species, as had been thought, the quagga was found to be a subspecies, with DNA identical to that of the still-living plains zebra. Since its coat pattern, with stripes mostly on the front section and plain brown hindquarters, turned out to be the only perceptible difference between quaggas and their surviving cousins, Rau believed that re-bred animals that looked like quaggas could justifiably be called quaggas.

Determined to rectify a tragic mistake, Rau decided to try resurrecting the creature, launching the Quagga Project in 1987. Nine plains zebra with quagga-like traits were captured in Etosha National Park and selectively bred. The progress of the Rau quaggas in just 30 years is significant. While it will never be possible to put right the extinction of a species, the Quagga Project is a small step in the right direction.

27

THE VAN OUDTSHOORN VAULT

The last remnant of Baron van Oudtshoorn's estate

5 Faure Street
Daily during office hours (ring the bell at the gate to request access)
Free entry

Tucked away in the backyard of an old-age home is a lonely tomb – the sole remainder of the once large and grand estate of an old Cape family. Baron Pieter van Rheede van Oudtshoorn tot Nederhorst arrived at the Cape in 1741, first as fiscal independent and then deputy governor for the Dutch East India Company (VOC). In 1743 he was granted a prime parcel of land between Hof and Kloof Streets, which he named Oudtshoorn Gardens.

In 1791, his wealthy son William Ferdinand, who also worked for the VOC, appointed the famous French architect Louis Michel Thi-

bault to design a fine homestead on Kloof Street, which was named Saasveld. Decorations were done by the well-known sculptor Anton Anreith. When the Cape became a British protectorate four years later, William Ferdinand was the only member of the council who refused to swear allegiance to the British crown.

Although the estate was subdivided into three separate properties, including the Mount Nelson (where the hotel today stands), the homestead survived until 1957, when it was demolished by the Dutch Reformed Church to build a youth hostel. However, each brick was numbered and transported to Franschhoek, where it was rebuilt and opened as the Huguenot Museum in 1967.

Within the whitewashed vault, which was also designed by Thibault and is now a national monument, lie Baron William Ferdinand van Reede van Oudtshoorn (1755–1822) and his wives Susanna van Schoor (died 1776) and Gezina Kirsten (died 1817).

The Pickled Baron

In 1766 Baron Pieter retired from the VOC and returned to Europe. However, after the Prince of Orange appointed him Governor of the Cape, the baron boarded the ship *Asia* bound for the Cape on 4 January 1773. He fell ill shortly after setting sail and died a few days later on 23 January.

Usually, people who died aboard a ship would be buried at sea. But the baron was placed in a lead-lined coffin that he happened to have brought with him on the journey. The story goes that the ship's captain filled the coffin with brandy to preserve the body, as it would take the ship another three months to reach Cape Town. The baron was given a state funeral and buried in the Groote Kerk in Adderley Street on 17 April. When the church was enlarged, his gravestone was removed from its original position in the pavement and is now mounted on the eastern wall.

The town of Oudtshoorn is named after Baron Pieter, although he never went there. The husband of the baron's granddaughter Ernestina was Egbertus Bergh, one of the founding fathers of the town.

THE UBUNTU TREE

28

A magical tree renowned for its spiritual healing properties

99 Kloof Street
Free entry

In the courtyard of the Cape Town Medi-Spa behind the Mount Nelson is an old Banyan fig believed by spiritualists to have healing powers. The tree is thought to be over 400 years old. Along with the two trees growing on either side, it marks the edge of what was once Weltevreden Dam, a natural pond fed by the streams of Camissa, which run from Table Mountain (the water was long ago sent underground, and the dam is remembered only by a nearby street name).

Banyan trees are sacred in both Hindu and Buddhist mythologies, but visitors to this tree come from a diverse range of backgrounds. The Maasai activist Miyere Ole Miyandazi made a pilgrimage to the tree when he reached Cape Town after walking from Kenya, as did Credo Mutwa, the famous Zulu sangoma and herbalist. Dr Masaru Emoto, the Japanese researcher who believes that human consciousness has an effect on the molecular structure of water, has also spent time with the tree. His photograph of the ubuntu water crystal can be seen in the Medi-Spa.

The tree was named Unabantu Nokuphila by local traditional healers. In Xhosa this means 'place of the healing mother where the people gather for health and wellness.' It is affectionately known as 'The Ubuntu Tree'. Visitors to the courtyard are welcome and encouraged to spend time beneath its branches in meditation and contemplation. You can also follow the Ubuntu Tree on Facebook.

OTHER NOTABLE TREES NEARBY
The Slave Tree Plaque in Spin Street
On the traffic island opposite Church Square is a circular granite plaque commemorating the site of the Slave Tree. This is where slaves were apparently auctioned and where they would have waited for their masters attending services at the Groote Kerk. Slavery was abolished in 1834 and the original fir tree was removed in 1916.

The Saffron Pear Tree in the Company's Garden
Probably the oldest cultivated tree in South Africa, the saffron pear tree in the Company's Garden was brought here from Holland during the time of Jan van Riebeeck. One of the original varieties of pear, *Pyrus communis*, it is known as the common pear or saffron pear. Traditionally, the leaves were used to dye wool saffron yellow and the fruits were used in pickles and preserves. The tree's original trunk collapsed many years ago and what remains are four sprouts that emerged from the roots. The ancient branches are held up by metal crutches and cables and protected by a fence. In 2013, cuttings were taken to preserve the tree's genetic material.

MOLTENO POWER STATION

Cape Town's first municipal power station

Corner of Molteno Road and Belvedere Avenue
Closed to the public

Although the streets of Kimberley were already lit by electricity in 1882, it was more than a decade later, at 7:30pm on 13 April 1895, that Mayoress Smart switched on Cape Town's electric street lights. Earlier that day, Mayor George Smart had inaugurated the generating station that powered the lights by breaking a bottle of Champagne against one of the turbines. The Graaff Electrical Lighting Works on the banks of the Molteno Reservoir was Cape Town Municipality's first power station and the first hydroelectric station in South Africa.

The driving force behind the power station, and the man after whom it was named, was Sir David de Villiers Graaff, mayor of Cape Town from 1891 to 1892 and member of parliament until 1897. Lawrence Green wrote that Graaff had tried for years to convince the city council to illuminate the streets by means of electricity. (Cape Town had gas lighting after the first gasworks opened in 1845.)

The first cables for electrification were laid in January 1894 and the network was completed in 15 months, with a total of 775 street lights throughout the city and Three Anchor Bay. To power them, the Cape Town City Council commissioned two 150kW generators that could be driven by steam or water (the chimney stack has since been removed). The cost of the power station, paid for by Graaff himself, was £75,000.

The *Cape Argus* reported: "Cape Town is ahead of many towns in Britain in adopting this mysterious force, the electric fluid."

The power station was closed in 1920 and declared a national monument in 1993. The area around the reservoir is open for public recreation.

Cape Town's Electrical Milestones

1860 – The first electric telegraph system is introduced, between Cape Town and Simon's Town.

1882 – Electric lighting is installed in parliament and an arc-lighting installation is commissioned in the harbour.

1891 – Mr George Pigot Moodie sets up a private lighting installation at his home in Rondebosch, which powers the first electric street light in the Cape at Rondebosch Fountain.

1895 – The Graaff Electric Lighting Works is inaugurated.

1896 – The first electric tram service runs from Adderley Street to Mowbray.

1904 – Cape Town's second power station is opened in Dock Road.

1923 – The Electricity Supply Commission (Eskom) is established.

1966 – Table Mountain is lit up with floodlights for the first time to mark the republic's fifth anniversary.

THE HURLING PUMP

A relic of the days when slaves collected water

Corner of Prince and Sir George Grey Streets

The little pump-house at the corner of Prince and Sir George Grey Streets is a very different sort of building from the other houses in this wealthy neighbourhood. It is the sole surviving remnant of one of the many attempts made in Cape Town's history to resolve its water-supply problems.

Even as late as the 19th century, Capetonians still had to fetch all their household water from public fountains on the Grand Parade and Greenmarket Square. In fact, most well-to-do households owned a slave whose chief responsibility was the fetching and carrying of water. This system not only resulted in a great deal of wasted time, but, since the fountains ran continuously, also wasted drinking water – a resource that was becoming increasingly scarce.

In order to relieve the congestion at the fountains and save water, in 1812 Governor Sir John Cradock gave the Burgher Senate a grant to provide a new water system for Cape Town. The improvements included the construction of several swinging pumps (swaaipompe) around the city. Water was captured in reservoirs on the slopes of the mountain, then led into wells by means of wooden waterways and pipes. Above each well, a pump-house was built, with a long, weighted wooden handle that the slaves worked by swinging from side to side.

Because this pump is known as the 'Hurling Swaai Pump', the invention of the mechanism is sometimes attributed to Jan Frederick Hurling, a prominent Swedish colonist in Cape Town at the time. However, it seems more likely that this particular pump got its name from the fact that it was situated on Hurling's farm, Zorgvliet, which he bought in 1791.

The pump-house, with its somewhat comical conical spire, was probably designed by the Cape's most popular architect of that era, Louis Michel Thibault; the bronze face from which the water would have spouted is almost certainly the work of Thibault's frequent collaborator, Anton Anreith. There is some debate as to whether the gargoyle represents a lion or a water sprite, or perhaps even the northwesterly wind that brings Cape Town's rain. It's presumed that the slate above the spout would have been used to record the amount of water consumed.

Despite the fact that few residents ever even notice it, the Hurling pump has been a national monument since 1937.

THE STADTSFONTEIN

The city's original water source

Homestead Park
Upper Orange Street

While the Castle and the Company's Garden are widely regarded as the starting point of the Cape colony, it is, in fact, a forgotten field in Oranjezicht that furnished the foundation for Cape Town's development. The 13 perennial springs, known collectively as the Stadtsfontein (City Fountain), that emerge here provided the single most important source of fresh water for the early settlement. Known by the original Quena inhabitants as Camissa, meaning 'place of sweet waters', it was the only perennial water source on the face of the mountain and formed the lifeblood of the city for more than two centuries.

The springs' water flowed through 'leiwaters' to irrigate the Company's Garden; it was diverted around the Castle as a moat, channelled through open canals or 'grachts', piped into public pumps and fountains, and stored in dams and reservoirs. In 1719, the Stadtsfontein became part of a farm established by Pieter van Breda. The remains of the farm can still be seen at Homestead Park. In the 1800s, the Dutch built structures around the springs to protect them.

However, when the bubonic plague broke out in Cape Town in 1901,

the canals were covered over and the springs were sent underground. By then, the city's demand had outgrown its supply, so water was brought from elsewhere – first from dams built on top of Table Mountain and eventually all the way from Franschoek. The city's original water source was neglected to such an extent that in 1990 the Stadtsfontein springs were scrapped from the city's asset resource register.

The springs still gush more than 3.5 million litres of potential drinking water every day. A fraction of it is now being used to irrigate the Green Point Park, but most of it runs straight into the sea. Despite concerns about future water shortages, dozens of ingenious proposals and almost a decade of debate, no plans are in place to properly utilise this resource. The Stadtsfontein remains entirely overlooked, behind a barbed wire fence and permanently padlocked gate. Only faint reminders of its former significance endure in street names such as Mill Street, Buitengracht and Heerengracht.

"Don't Shit in the Water"

The Stadtsfontein even gave rise to the nation's first environmental law, Placcaat 12 of 1655, which stated: "Niet boven de stroom van de spruitjie daer de schepen haer water halen te wassen en deselve troubel te maken." This was famously summarised as: "Moenie in die water kak nie" (Don't shit in the water).

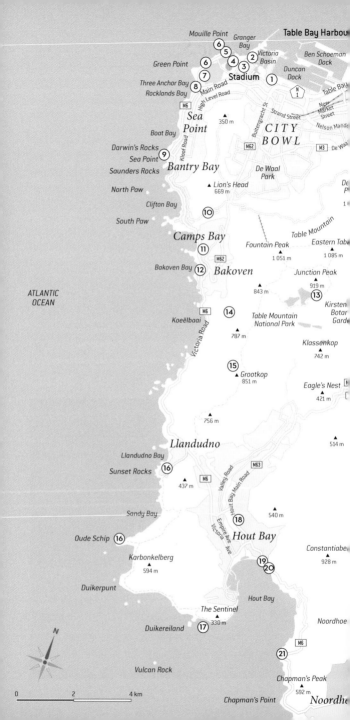

Atlantic Seaboard

SHIP SOCIETY

Step back into maritime history

Opposite F-berth
Duncan Road, Cape Town Harbour
philsh@telkomsa.net (Philip Short) or brupa@telkomsa.net (Pauline Brueton)
Meetings every Thursday at 7pm
Also open on Saturday afternoons

Founded in 1953, the Ship Society of South Africa gathers every Thursday night at 7pm to celebrate all things nautical. Meetings take place in a small clubhouse building in Duncan Dock and non-members are welcome. The clubhouse, with its model ships and nautical memorabilia, is well worth a visit by anyone attracted to the ocean.

The Ship Society is a little-known Cape Town institution that seeks to bring together all those interested in the South African shipping and maritime industries for social events, DVDs and talks by guest speakers. The rooms are also open on Saturday afternoons for informal meetings and an opportunity to browse its library of maritime books, photographs, videos and journals.

The society aims to maintain the rich heritage of South African shipping and promote the idea that our maritime legacy is intricately linked to the development of the country.

The 1950s were the heyday of ocean liners. Known as the Tavern of the Seas, Cape Town was a well-established port with vessels of many nations calling on a regular basis. During this period, a group of nautical enthusiasts used to bump into each other on the quayside, cameras poised to capture the docked vessels. In 1953 they banded together to form the Ship Society and began holding regular meetings in the crypt of St George's Cathedral. Membership grew steadily and, when more space was needed, meetings moved to the Union Castle building in the city centre.

In 1971 the society moved again to Thibault Square, after which it secured rooms at the original Port Captain's building at the Pierhead in the V&A Harbour. Along with the new rooms came custodianship of the Clock Tower, which housed the society's growing collection of model ships, pictures and crockery.

The development of the modern V&A Waterfront compelled the society to move to new premises in Duncan Dock. The current building was constructed in 1942 and was initially used as a naval headquarters – HMSAS Bonaventure, better known as Bon 1.

After World War II, Bon 1 was vacated but the buildings were retained by the navy. In 1955 it became an administration block responsible for Coastal Command's various gun batteries. The site was eventually handed over to South African Railways and Harbours, and in 1990, the Ship Society moved in.

JETTY 1

An intense reminder of a heart-rending apartheid experience

Quay 5, V&A Waterfront
Daily 7am–5.30pm
Free entry

Every year, thousands of people board the ferry from the V&A Waterfront to visit the political landmark that is Robben Island. But as they depart from the gleaming Robben Island Exhibition and Information Centre, few of them are aware that the official embarkation point – the start and end of all the journeys taken by Robben Island's prisoners themselves – actually lies across the harbour in a small, nondescript building on Jetty 1. For 30 years, everyone travelling to and from Robben Island, whether prisoner, visitor, warder or staff member, passed through these premises. The site bears the footprints of hundreds of political and common-law prisoners, their families and visitors, waiting to sail towards a feared destination.

Jetty 1 is now a national monument and the former embarkation building houses a small, usually empty, museum. You can sit on the hard beds in one of the old holding cells, or on the empty benches in the visitors' waiting room where the walls are plastered with copies of applications for visitor's permits – some with a large, careless 'OK' scrawled across them. The permits bear the following instructions: "The boat leaves Cape Town docks at 1:30pm and returns at 4:00pm. No children under the age of 16 years are allowed to visit their relatives on the island." Barred windows look out onto sparkling water, Waterfront shoppers and a lazily turning ferris wheel.

Originally known as the east jetty, Jetty 1 was the first to be built in the Victoria Basin. It was, in fact, closely associated with Robben Island long before the advent of apartheid. Constructed by Robben Island prisoners in the 19th century, it was the original embarkation point for the island, which was then used as a British convict station and hospital.

In 1925 a portion of Jetty 1 was cordoned off for the exclusive use of Robben Island – official Robben Island Offices were constructed on it in 1957. When the island was declared a maximum-security prison and handed over to Prison Services in 1961, Jetty 1 became the sole embarkation point for Robben Island. The original building of corrugated zinc and iron sheeting was demolished in the 70s and replaced with the current brick building. In 1988, the offices were renamed the Prisons Department Offices. Robben Island's last political prisoners were released in 1991, but the common-law prison was only closed in 1996. Interestingly, the V&A Waterfront opened in 1990, so for a time, the luxury shopping mall and maximum-security prison facility must have shared an uneasy coexistence.

BREAKWATER PRISON TREADMILL ③

A cruel hamster wheel for humans

UCT Graduate School of Business
Northern parking lot, University of Cape Town, 8 Portswood Road
V&A Waterfront

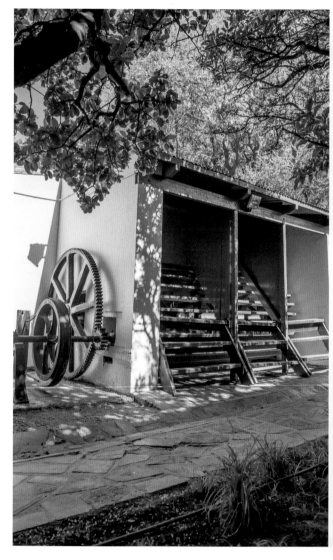

The Breakwater Prison treadmill sits beside the solitary-confinement cells in a parking lot at the University of Cape Town's Business School. It is thought to be unique in sub-Saharan Africa.

Convicts who caused trouble could either be thrown into solitary confinement or sentenced to hours, sometimes even days, on the treadmill.

For 55 minutes of every hour, a convict would hang onto an overhead bar while his feet kept the treadmill turning at a steady pace. It was like a cruel hamster wheel for humans. Should the prisoner slack off, the wooden treads would crack him on the shins until they bled.

Beside the treadmill you'll find the row of isolation cells and two death cells. Gallows Hill, used for executions, is less than a kilometre away and is the current location of Cape Town's Traffic Department.

Also adjacent to the treadmill stands the wall of the original prison. It's scored with Anglo-Boer War graffiti carved in the stone by inmates and shows images of President Paul Kruger, Cecil John Rhodes and celebrations at the fall of Mafeking in 1902.

Just below the prison is a quarry that was excavated for its rock. Today, the V&A Marina and One & Only Hotel stand on the edge of the flooded quarry. Prisoners hauled the rock up the hill in rail wagons, then down through a tunnel beside Dock House to be used in the construction of the harbour's breakwater.

Many convicts were guilty of no more than having jumped ship at the Cape. They'd been press-ganged into maritime service in England and found life at sea too hard to bear.

The old Breakwater Gaol was a prominent feature on Cape Town's shoreline long before Robben Island achieved worldwide notoriety as a prison. There were, in fact, two breakwater jails, the first of which was built in 1859, when construction of the breakwater for the Victoria & Alfred Basins commenced. After a strike in 1885, when black and white convicts held meetings in the yard together, prison authorities decided that interracial contact was causing the trouble and decided to segregate prisoners.

The Industrial Breakwater Prison (today housing the Graduate School of Business) was built in 1901 to incarcerate white male convicts. The design of four castellated turrets and an enclosed courtyard was based on that of Millbank and Pentonville prisons in England. It was only used as a jail for 10 years.

DISAPPEARING GUN

The only 9.2-inch disappearing gun in Africa

Next to the Cape Town Stadium on a bluff opposite the intersection of Beach and Haul Roads, Granger Bay
Fort Wynyard is currently closed to the public, but the gun is visible from Beach Road

Driving towards the V&A Waterfront along Beach Road, you'll notice a curious white protrusion peeping above a low ridge on the landward side. This is the barrel of Africa's only disappearing gun and one of the last of its kind in the world.

During the early 19th century, the British strengthened the defences of Table Bay with a number of gun emplacements. Set after 1862 alongside with other new artillery pieces, the 9.2-inch disappearing gun is the centrepiece of Fort Wynward.

The fort was constructed either alongside or on top of an 18th-century VOC battery called Kyk in de Pot (Look in the Pot) built by the Dutch. The name refers to the fact that the guns overlooked a whaling station housing huge blubber pots.

Fort Wynyard continued to be used well into the 20th century; it was active during World War I and II and today it's both a military museum (closed to the general public) and home to the Cape Garrison Artillery.

The disappearing gun is a fibreglass replica because the weight of the 26-ton original (now located at the entrance to the fort) was beginning to damage its wooden block mount.

What is a disappearing gun?

These guns were invented in the 1860s as heavy artillery pieces in which the carriage enabled the gun to rotate backwards and down into a pit protected by a parapet after it was fired. This lowered the gun from view while it was being reloaded. With the gun in a retracted position, the battery was much harder to spot from the sea, making it a difficult target for attacking ships. In addition, flat trajectory fire tended to fly over the top of the battery without damaging it. The retracting system also made reloading easier, as it lowered the breech to a level where shells could simply be rolled up to it for loading and ramming.

Although the gun had some avantages, the disappearating carriage was a complicated and expansive mechanism. Moreover, their firing angle was often limitated. Though effective against ships, it turned out to be vulnerable to attack from the air. By 1912, these guns were declared obsolete in the British Army.

REMAINS OF THE MOUILLE POINT ⑤ LIGHTHOUSE

The obsolete lighthouse

Cape Town Hotel School car park, 3 Beach Road, Mouille Point.
Entrance is free: walk past the barriers into the car park and turn right. The
base of the lighthouse is near the terrace of the Hotel School Restaurant

Completed in 1842, Mouille Point Light was the second lighthouse in South Africa. It was operational until 1908, when the Table Bay Harbour breakwater light was built. Today, all that remains of the original Mouille Point Lighthouse is the four-metre high, brick and slate base, situated in the grounds of the Hotel School of the Cape Peninsula University of Technology in Granger Bay. This is also the former site of the old Mouille Point Battery.

The name 'mouille' comes from the French for anchorage or mooring. In the early 18th century, wrecks were common in Table Bay and the Cape governor decided that a breakwater ('moeilje' in Dutch) was needed to shelter vessels.

Work began in 1743 and all farmers delivering goods to the city were required to load their wagons with stones, drive to Mouille Point and offload. Primarily slaves and convicts were used to build the breakwater, but after three years of hard labour and high seas, only 100 metres had been built and the project was abandoned. In 1781, the French arrived, and constructed a gun emplacement near the unfinished breakwater, naming it Mouille Point Battery.

Built on the same site, the lighthouse was an elegant structure, about 11 metres tall and comprising a cylindrical brick tower with a gallery and an octagonal lantern imported from Paris. A four-metre hollow foundation in the bedrock provided for oil storage. The tower was plastered, painted with red and white bands and had a dioptric lamp which used about 730 gallons of sheep-tail oil per year.

The Mouille Point Lighthouse sadly failed to meet the stringent requirements of naval captains entering and leaving Table Bay. Many regarded the light as too dim and easily confused with shore lights. Indeed, during its lifetime, a number of ships ran aground on the rocks in front of it. The most notable of these was the RMS *Athens*, wrecked with all hands just below the light, during the great gale of 1865. The tower was decommissioned on 15 April 1908 and demolished soon after.

Today's famous Green Point Lighthouse, a beautiful red-and-white structure near the site of the old lighthouse, is often erroneously referred to as the Mouille Point Lighthouse.

RMS *ATHENS* WRECK

The great gale and the loss of the RMS Athens

The engine block of the RMS Athens *protrudes above the waves off Mouille Point*
Parking lot at the intersection of Beach Road and Fritz Sonnenberg Road
Information about the wreck can be found on a board next to the parking lot

The tragic wreck of the Royal Mail Ship *Athens* took place on the night of 17 May 1865. This 739-ton, 68-metre barque of the Union Line, built in 1856, was commanded by David Smith, who had taken over the captaincy just two days earlier. With a crew of 30, the RMS *Athens* was employed in the mail run between Southampton and Cape Town for six years.

She was wrecked at Mouille Point while trying to steam out of Table Bay during the 'great gale' of 1865. This infamous storm, the most destructive in the Cape's history, resulted in the loss of 19 ships. The *Athens* had been at anchor in the bay, preparing to leave for Mauritius. Her last anchor cable parted at about 6pm and Captain Smith headed out to sea in an attempt to ride out the storm in deeper water.

As the vessel rounded Mouille Point she was hammered by heavy swells. Her engine, producing a mere 130hp, made painstakingly slow progress. It's thought that her boiler fires may have been extinguished by enormous waves and she drifted towards the shore.

By 8pm the ship had been driven broadside onto the rocks. Green Point residents assembled on the beach with lights, ropes and lifebuoys, but the foul weather meant that no rescue was possible. Cries of distress came from the ship, but these had ceased by about 9:30pm.

A contemporary eyewitness account, published in the *Cape Argus* newspaper, describes the scene at 10pm: "The ship was lying sixty or eighty yards from the shore, grinding heavily on the rocks with every sea, and evidently fast breaking up, for pillow cases and cabin doors were washing ashore, so as to leave no doubt that the wreck was complete. No dead bodies could, however, be found on the beach, but in the face of the tremendous seas and the boiling surf, it appeared impossible that any single one of the unfortunate people on board could reach the shore alive."

Twenty-eight men died in the freezing Atlantic waters that night. The second and third officers escaped with their lives as they'd been ashore during the day and were unable to return to the ship due to the bad weather. Today, all that is visible of the RMS *Athens* is her engine block, standing tall about 50 metres offshore in the surf off Mouille Point.

The only living creature to survive the wreck was a pig that managed to swim ashore.

THE GRAND VLEI

Site of the former yachting regattas of Green Point Common

Green Point Urban Park
The golf-course lake is situated on the east side of the path separating the biodiversity garden from the golf course
Daily from sunrise to sunset

Green Point Urban Park is a delightful place for a family picnic and for children to explore and play. There's a lovely, newly built lake between the park and the golf course that harks back to the large pond situated here during the 19th century.

A natural depression in the common would fill with water in the winter and sailing regattas were held on this shallow, seasonal vlei. It became so popular that young sailors established the Green Point Amateur Boat and Canoe Club in 1887. In 1889 the municipality deepened and extended the pond by raising the banks and redirecting storm water. The Grand Vlei became a sizeable lake nearly two kilometres in circumference and two metres deep.

The highlight of each year was Regatta Day, held in early September. Club members wore uniforms of white duck trousers, blue jackets and caps bearing the club badge. Boats for these regattas were built at a nearby workshop in Three Anchor Bay. The Juritz brothers had a thriving business in wooden sailing dinghies.

After a decade, the vlei was drained and filled in to prevent stagnant water from becoming a health hazard to the military and the Boer POW camps established during the Anglo-Boer War of 1899-1902.

Cape Town's Commonage

There is a long history of public recreation on the coastal plain of Green Point Common. *De vlakte genaamdt de Groene Punt* has been a public open space since the establishment of the Cape settlement in 1652. During the 18th century, the Green Point Common was known by the Dutch as *De Waterplaats* (the Foreshore) and extended from Three Anchor Bay all the way to town. In 1862 the first rugby match in South Africa took place between army officers and gentlemen of the civil service at Green Point Common. The match ended in a 0-0 draw.

In 1900 the golfing fraternity persuaded the authorities to make land available for a golf course. With some alteration in layout, the course still occupies a substantial portion of the commonage today. Regular horse races were held on the common and the building that today houses McDonalds was the original grandstand. The slopes of Signal Hill also accommodated spectators. In addition, the common was the venue for some of the Cape's earliest cricket matches, while the Green Point Track was an important place for cycling and other field sports.

CITY KAYAKING AT THREE ANCHOR BAY

Some of the Cape's finest views

Three Anchor Bay beach
Kaskazi rents out kayaks at 179 Beach Road
083-346-1146
kayak.co.za

Three Anchor Bay is an ideal city location from which to launch a kayak and explore the Table Bay coastline. Paddle north around Green Point to Granger Bay or south towards Clifton Beach and you'll be treated to some of the Cape's finest views.

There's prolific bird life on the rocks and in the water, with various species of nesting cormorants, seagulls, terns and gannets, as well as African penguins making the occassional appearance. Seals and dolphins often cruise along beside the kayaks. If you're lucky, you might encounter southern right or humpback whales, especially during winter and spring.

At the fuel station beside the beach, there's a shop that sells and rents out kayaks, as well as offering day tours on the water. The kayaks are stored in boathouses tucked beneath the promenade above the beach.

The Suicide of Ingrid Jonker

Ingrid Jonker was a liberal Afrikaans poet considered to be 'the Sylvia Plath of South Africa'. In the early hours of 19 July 1965, at the age of 31, Jonker walked into the sea at Three Anchor Bay and committed suicide by drowning.

Although Jonker wrote in Afrikaans, her poems have been widely translated. Her sensitive and progressive outlook has made her a literary icon for a new generation of South Africans who've rediscovered her relevance.

Jonker's conservative father was chairman of a parliamentary committee responsible for censorship laws. To his great embarrassment, Ingrid was strongly opposed to these laws and he publicly disowned her.

The poet led a tempestuous life and had many affairs, notably with two well-known writers, André Brink and Jack Cope. One of these liaisons resulted in a pregnancy and subsequent abortion. The mental distress of the abortion and her father's rejection contributed to Jonker entering Valkenberg Psychiatric Hospital in 1961.

Her second volume of poetry brought her wide acclaim. She became part of Die Sestigers, a group of writers who sought to challenge the conservative Afrikaans literary establishment.

By early 1965 Ingrid was on medication, drinking heavily and experiencing another breakdown. Just before her death, she witnessed a scene in which a black baby was shot in his mother's arms. Nelson Mandela read her poem '*Die Kind Wat Doodgeskiet is Deur Soldate by Nyanga*' (The Child Who Was Shot Dead by Soldiers at Nyanga) during his address at the opening of South Africa's first democratically elected parliament in 1994.

CHARLES DARWIN'S ROCKS ⑨

Rocks recorded by Charles Darwin in Sea Point

Parking lot at the south end of Queens Beach near the intersection of Beach and Alexander Roads in Sea Point
Look over the edge of the Sea Point promenade and note the different colours in the rocks below
A plaque on the Sea Point promenade provides the history

Whenever there's a decent swell, surfers clamber over a group of curious, streaky-coloured rocks at the south end of Queens Beach before leaping into the waves. These rocks were visited by Charles Darwin in 1836 during his epic voyage around the world on HMS *Beagle*.

A plaque in the parking lot commemorates Darwin's observation that this intrusion of basaltic volcanic rock into granitic rock was a unique geological feature. The plaque also includes a drawing of the *Beagle* and quotes from his work.

The rocks reveal an impressive contact zone of dark slate with pale intrusive granite. This interesting example of contact between sedimentary and igneous rock was first recorded by Clarke Abel in 1818. It shows how, about 540 million years ago, molten granite intruded into the older, darker, metamorphosed siltstone of the Malmesbury Group of rocks. Although this intrusion initially occurred at great depth, prolonged erosion eventually exposed the granite, forming a basement onto which younger sedimentary rocks of the Table Mountain Group were deposited. This contact was influential in understanding the geology of the Earth.

Darwin's later account of the rocks at Sea Point (which he erroneously called 'Green Point') was a result of eight years of writing and correspondence after his return to England.

The rocks were proclaimed a historical monument in 1953 and a bronze plaque was erected by the National Monuments Council. In 2010 the plaque was stolen for its metal and the City of Cape Town replaced it with an informative plaque describing the significance of the outcrops. Even this new plaque, made of synthetic material, has been vandalised in an abortive attempt to steal it for its 'metal' content.

"A man must for years examine for himself great piles of superimposed strata, and watch the sea at work grinding down old rocks and making fresh sediment, before he can hope to comprehend anything about the lapse of time, the monuments of which we see around us."
Charles Darwin, *The Origin of Species*, 1859

ROUNDHOUSE

A 'secret romance' at the shooting box

Round House Road (off Kloof Road)
Camps Bay
021-438-4347

The Roundhouse is an attractive building set in a leafy corner of the Glen on the slopes of Lion's Head. Over the centuries, it has performed many functions, but most famously as Lord Charles Somerset's hunting lodge.

Due to its strategic location, this site was chosen as a guardhouse in 1786 by the Dutch East India Company. With sweeping views of the Atlantic, it was ideally situated to safeguard Cape Town from a seaborne landing.

Lord Charles Somerset, governor of the Cape from 1814 to 1827, was famous for his extravagance. He enlarged, renovated and refurbished the structure, converting it into a hunting lodge. The alterations were paid for by the British Government, which gave rise to considerable discontent among settlers.

Somerset added a veranda around the curved structure and fitted fashionable French windows. After its improvements, the Roundhouse boasted a saloon, a hall, three bedrooms, a kitchen, and three rooms on the lower storey, along with slave lodgings. After a day out hunting leopards and antelope on the slopes of Table Mountain, Somerset and his guests would retire to this opulent 'shooting box'.

Somerset's departure in 1827 didn't mean the end of hospitality at the Roundhouse. In 1848, Kloof Road was built, making Camps Bay more accessible to Capetonians. Since the mid-19th century, the Roundhouse has operated periodically as a tearoom, dance hall, hotel, and a restaurant (its current incarnation).

There are many legends about the building, none more intriguing than that of Doctor James Barry. One of Lord Somerset's great friends and his family physician, Barry often called at the Roundhouse. Their friendship became the subject of hushed conversation concerning the possibility of a homosexual affair.

Despite Barry's shrill voice and strange appearance, he was a brilliant surgeon and is credited with performing the first Caesarean section in Africa. Yet the most astonishing aspect about Barry wasn't revealed until his death. After succumbing to infection in 1865, the nurse who laid out his body revealed that he was, in fact, a woman.

Barry's legacy lives on as the Roundhouse's 'lady of the manor'. It is said that her soul still roams the grounds. Some even claim to have seen her ghostly figure dressed in military garb or riding through the Glen on horseback.

ROTUNDA

The grande dame of Camps Bay

69 Victoria Road (at the rear of The Bay Hotel)
Camps Bay
021-430-4444

Flanked by tall palm trees, the Rotunda is a majestic, geometrical, domed structure that hosted turn-of-the-century high society. Built in 1904, it started life as part of a hotel and became a popular functions venue. The high-ceilinged, circular structure has a raised stage and a large chandelier at its centre. Today, it serves as a venue for weddings, fashion shows, corporate events and the like.

The history of the Rotunda, now part of The Bay Hotel, dates back to 1901. Unofficial mayor of Camps Bay, James Riddell Farquhar, devised a plan to transform the bay from a sleepy residential hollow into a holiday resort. It was Farquhar who planted the iconic row of palm trees along the beachfront to make Camps Bay resemble 'Little Brighton'. His makeover gave birth to the Rotunda.

It was established as a concert hall with a pavilion that, over the decades, served variously as a ballroom, theatre, exhibition hall, roller-skating rink and a venue for church services. Even boxing matches were held there.

Suzanne Krige fondly remembers coming to dances at the Rotunda during World War II. "When I was a student, we used to drive through from the southern suburbs to Camps Bay on Saturday nights. The band on the stage would play big-band favourites, especially Glen Miller. It was simply magical."

By the 1950s, the Rotunda had passed into the hands of the Satz Brothers, who planned to demolish it and build a seven-storey block of flats in its place. Residents protested, claiming that the development would not only destroy a fine Florentine-style building, but their view of the bay would be blocked. As a result of their action, a three-storey height restriction for all buildings was enforced in the area.

The site was rezoned and expropriated by the Cape Town City Council and the building was saved from demolition. Later, modern additions to the Rotunda (built in the 1950s by SA Breweries) were torn down and the older section was incorporated into The Bay Hotel. The Rotunda was declared a national monument in 1974.

BETA BEACH

Hideaway beach, a scuba-diving heaven

Bakoven
Parking lot on Beta Close, off Beta Road, Bakoven
Follow the path down to the beach

The small suburb of Bakoven ('baking oven' in Dutch) is probably named after an offshore rock in the shape of a traditional wood-burning oven. The village is made up of coastal bungalows and cottages tucked against the shore with more luxurious penthouse apartments and high-end homes further up the slope.

Bakoven Beach (also known as Beta Beach) is tiny and almost non-existent at spring high tide. This picturesque strip of white sand is surrounded by granite boulders and a handful of cottages. Being relatively protected from the southeaster, it's a great place for secluded sunbathing, rock-pool exploring and kayaking. The backdrop of the Twelve Apostles adds to the already dramatic view of the bay. The boulders to the west of the beach are good for sundowners.

The underwater world here is also spectacular, so bring along a wetsuit, mask and snorkel. If you're a scuba diver, Bakoven Rock is a fine spot. The best place to enter the water is either at the concrete ramp used by rescue boats or at any suitable point in the cove to the west of Beta Beach.

There's a rocky bottom and kelp forests in the shallower areas, while further out, the white quartz sand makes for great visibility. You'll find a wide variety of invertebrate reef life, particularly on the sheltered vertical and overhanging faces. It's a great area for macro photography of invertebrates. A spotlight is useful for looking into crevices and a compass will help you find your way back at the end of the dive.

When there's a westerly swell running, the surge here can be strong. The spot works best during or after southeasterly winds, or when the swell is mild. The site is usually at its best in summer, but there are occasional opportunities throughout the year.

NEARBY
Other dive sites

Less than two kilometres north of Bakoven, and 100 metres offshore, lies Clifton Rock. It encompasses an area of large boulders, creating swimthroughs and sheltered spots for marine life, including nudibranches, starfish, soft sponges and various crustaceans.

Another great site lies three kilometres southwest of Bakoven at Oudekraal. Coral Gardens is a rocky reef and the landscape both above and below the water is dominated by large granite boulders. There are plenty of overhangs, crevices and small caves, with occasional swimthroughs. The site is famed for its noble coral (*Allopora nobilis*).

THE BEACH ON TOP OF TABLE MOUNTAIN

A white-sand beach where you'd least expect to find one

Start from Kirstenbosch Botanical Gardens
Daily 8am–6pm

Although Cape Town is famed for its soft, white-sand beaches, there's one that only the most energetic visitors ever get to see. That's because this beach is on top of Table Mountain, in a place only accessible through some strenuous hiking. Those who make the climb up Skeleton Gorge to take off their hiking boots and wiggle their toes in the sand on this peculiar beach can only wonder at how a perfect white-sand beach came to be on top of a mountain.

In fact, it's a man-made beach. But not the sort you'll find at land-locked holiday resorts. This beach wasn't created on purpose, but is the unlikely by-product of the dams that were built on what is called the 'back table' in the late 1800s (you can read more about their construction on page 104). The beach is at the far end of the huge Hely-Hutchinson Dam, which can hold nearly a billion litres of water, near where the Disa River flows into it.

As you may notice, Table Mountain sandstone (the predominant rock on the Cape Peninsula) is mostly grey in colour and is considered extremely weather resistant. However, you'll also notice that the water in the dam is a clear, bright orange. This tea colour is due to tannins: plant acids that leach into the water from the fynbos. Over time, the tannins have bleached the rocks that were submerged by the dam until they are almost pure white; they have also weakened and eroded them.

When the dam's water level drops and Cape Town's famous southeaster blows, the rock continues to erode into a white, powdery sand, which is blown into this sheltered corner. It's taken more than 100 years to create the beach and sand dunes, making this possibly the oldest, most time-consuming man-made beach in the world.

To reach the beach, take the Skeleton Gorge route up Table Mountain from Kirstenbosch Botanical Gardens. You can return the way you came, or walk along beside the dam and turn left to climb down via the Nursery Ravine route, which also starts in Kirstenbosch. It's also an easy walk across the Woodhead Dam wall to Kasteelspoort, where you can see the remains of the old cableway and enjoy great views of Camps Bay. Allow at least four hours for this hike.

KASTEELSPOORT CABLEWAY REMAINS

The location of Table Mountain's first cable car

Top of Kasteelspoort Ravine, Table Mountain National Park
Accessible between sunrise and sunset
Free entry

Plenty of people hike up Table Mountain via the Kasteelspoort route. Some will catch the modern cable car back down the mountain. However, very few are aware that Kasteelspoort was, in fact, the location of Table Mountain's first cable car, or that the remains of the old cable station are still there, just a few metres off the main hiking trail.

On reaching the top of Kasteelspoort Ravine, turn right at the direction marker towards the Twelve Apostles and Corridor Ravine trail. A few minutes later turn right again onto a small path leading directly to the northern edge of Postern Buttress. There you will find a large concrete platform with the rusty remains of the anchor points for the cableway on the edge of a rather breathtaking cliff.

The cable station's remains are almost the only evidence left of the work involved in one of Cape Town's most ambitious construction projects. Until the late 1880s the city managed on water from Table Mountain's rivers. But between 1890 and 1907 dams were built on top of Table Mountain to supply its growing water needs. Kasteelspoort offered the easiest access to these construction sites and long lines of porters toiled up it daily.

The Kasteelspoort cableway was built in 1893 to help haul equipment and building materials to the reservoirs. It was a small, open-skip, steam-driven cable car with its lower terminus above Camps Bay and its upper station 650 metres higher. Thanks to the cable station, a small town sprang up on top of the mountain, complete with a bank, post office and shop.

The first dam, Woodhead Reservoir, was completed in 1898. A year later, it became apparent that a second dam was needed. The construction of three more dams on the other side of the mountain was served by the Wynberg trolley track, of which no sign remains.

One of the Mountain's Most Spectacular Photo Opportunities

Near the remains of the anchor points for the cableway, at a spot aptly known as 'diving board rock', lies probably one of the mountain's most spectacular photo opportunities.

NEARBY
The Waterworks Museum
The museum is kept locked but you can arrange for someone to open it for you by phoning ahead with your planned visit date and estimated time of arrival
021-686-3408

Near the wall of the Hely-Hutchinson reservoir, accessible only by hikers, is a small stone building that houses memorabilia and equipment from the dams' construction, including a diminutive industrial steam locomotive. The locomotive transported materials from the cable station to the dams along a 2.6 km railway. Parts of the locomotive were brought up by the Kasteelspoort cable car, but the boiler was too big and heavy and had to be winched up the ravine on a wooden sledge, a process which took two weeks.

TRANQUILITY CRACKS

A notoriously difficult-to-find spot on the mountain

Table Mountain National Park
GPS S33°58.811; E18°23.012
Access between sunrise and sunset
Allow six to seven hours for the hike
Free entry

On top of the Twelve Apostles peaks above Camps Bay are a series of deep fissures in the Table Mountain sandstone. The cracks form a natural labyrinth of rock corridors, up to five metres deep in places, and stone pillars.

Once kept a closely guarded secret by elite local climbers, this spectacular hiking destination remains protected from the multitudes by its naturally hidden location, invisible until you're actually inside. In fact, even if you're standing right in front of the cracks with a GPS in your hand, the entrance may still elude you. Hikers who do manage to find Tranquility Cracks are likely to enjoy exploring them in solitude.

The easiest way to reach them is to start your hike on the Pipe Track, which can be accessed from the parking lot at the top of Kloof Nek Road. After about 40 minutes' walk, turn left and take the signposted Kasteelspoort route that leads to the summit of the mountain. At the top of this climb, turn right towards Corridor Ravine.

Walk for about 20 minutes along the trail and you'll ascend a small outcrop. Just a few metres past the top of this incline, try to spot the small cairn and the faint, overgrown trail to your right. If you reach Slangolie Ravine, you've gone too far. Follow this path as best you can towards the edge of the mountain and the rocky outcrop to your right. With a bit of skill – and plenty of luck – you'll find the gnarled yellowwood that guards the entrance to the cleft leading deep into the outcrop, which is known as Slangolie Face.

A grassy enclosure surrounded by tunnels branching into the contorted rock face makes the perfect place for a picnic, with views of the Apostles, the sharp needle of Lion's Head and Camps Bay far below.

For a different return route, after leaving Tranquility Cracks turn right as you regain the main path and continue away from Cape Town. Make your descent via Corridor Ravine and you will return to the Pipe Track a couple of kilometres further along from the Kasteelspoort trail. Take care not to descend via Woody Ravine, just before Corridor Ravine, as this is a dangerous route.

This is a full day's hike, and fairly strenuous, so allow at least six or seven hours and ensure all members of your group are fit. Remember to take sun hats, sunscreen, a warm jacket (no matter how hot the weather), enough energy food and plenty of water. Leave nothing behind but your footprints!

OUDESCHIP HIKE

*A spectacular trail rich in scenery
and history*

Start from the small parking lot on Sunset Avenue, Llandudno
Free entry

Let's be frank: many Capetonians avoid Sandy Bay. We're relatively prudish people, so our one and only nudist beach, despite its beauty, is seldom busy. And besides, the water is freezing. However, if you don't mind feeling somewhat overdressed, Sandy Bay is the starting point for a spectacular and surprisingly little-known hike.

From the Sandy Bay parking lot in Llandudno, walk along the path to the beach, then cross the sand to find a narrow path on your left leading up into a dense milkwood thicket. There are no signs and several dead ends, but keep close to the sea and you'll soon find the trail leading over the rocks towards the Oudeschip Peninsula. Look out for seals and whales.

About an hour's easy walking will bring you to the peninsula and the first shipwreck, the *Harvest Capella* (1986). If it's high tide you'll have to wade through icy water to reach it, so try to time your arrival for low tide so you can explore the rusted wreck and the rocks around it without

getting wet. This is an excellent spot for a picnic.

From the peninsula you'll also have a good view of the second shipwreck visible on this stretch of coastline: *Bos 400* (1994). This rather unusual wreck is that of a French crane barge that lost its towrope and ran aground in Maori Bay in heavy winter seas.

Ironically the bay is named after yet another ship wrecked there. At 1am on 5 August 1909, the SS *Maori*, carrying 2,300 tons of railway tracks, explosives, wine and Champagne, struck a rock off Duiker Point and sank with the loss of 32 lives. Her well-preserved remains are about 13 metres underwater. The wreck isn't visible to hikers, but it is a popular recreational diving site.

From Oudeschip you can return to Sandy Bay along the same path, or take the steep path up the mountain leading to a lookout hut. The hut was built in 1913 to store rescue equipment in case of another shipwreck, but it's now empty. From here you can turn right, continuing for another hour towards Maori Bay, or follow the path up, turning left onto the gravel road. At Sandy Bay Nek, a left turn will lead you back to Sandy Bay, where you can go for a refreshing skinny dip.

The hike takes three or four hours in total. Don't hike alone or become separated from your group. Unfortunately, robberies are regularly reported.

DUNGEONS SURF SPOT

Riding the biggest waves in Africa

Off Sentinal Peak, Hout Bay
View by boat from Hout Bay Harbour or from the shore (park in the suburb of Hangberg and hike over the hill to the west-facing slopes of Karbonkelberg)
The big wave only works on a few days each year

Dungeons is a big-wave surf spot that lies off the Sentinel, a monolithic peak that towers above Hout Bay. The wave is a right-hand reef break known for its power and ability to scare off all but the most experienced and daring surfers. It works best with a large, long-range groundswell from the southwest. One legendary session on 30 July 2006 saw tow-surfers tackle 60-foot waves – the biggest ridden in Africa at the time.

This fickle spot works typically as the result of a powerful winter storm. Only a handful of surfers dare to take on the terrifying wave. It's ridden by both conventional paddle-surfers and tow-surfers (where the rider is pulled into the waves behind a jet ski).

The nature of the spot makes it difficult to view. Your best bet is to monitor weather reports closely and keep checking websites such as

wavescape.co.za and windguru.cz. You need to be on the lookout for a well size of more than five metres combined with a swell period of over 15 seconds.

If you time the conditions right, your best chance of seeing these wave warriors is by either hitching a ride to the break on a boat from Hout Bay harbour (when the wave is big, a number of craft head out, many with photographers) or by watching from the land on the slopes of Karbonkelberg (take binoculars).

Dungeons was first surfed in 1984 when Peter Button and Pierre de Villiers braved the long paddle out through Shark Alley, teeming with seals and great white sharks. In the 1990s, another duo – Cass Collier and Ian Armstrong – began hitching a ride out to the break with local fishermen. In 1999, the Red Bull Big Wave Africa Contest was initiated and ran for a decade, popularising this spot.

Under ideal, windless conditions, with a swell of over 15 feet and a period of more than 20 seconds, Dungeons is awe-inspiring. Hillocks of water 775 metres long approach the coast at 35 metres per second (126 km/h). As they near the shore they jack up to 30 feet and begin toppling like imploding skyscrapers. This is the Cape of Storms at its most sublime.

THE EMPTY TABLE FOR TWO AT CAFÉ DEUS EX MACHINA

Kronendal's ghost

140 Main Road, Hout Bay
021-569-0625
Monday 7.30am–5pm; Tuesday–Saturday 7.30am–11pm;
Sunday 7.30am–7pm

When you visit Café Deus Ex Machina, you'll certainly appreciate the beautiful old building, elegant decor, good food and attentive service. As you enter the foyer you'll also notice that there is a table set for two. But there's nobody sitting at the table.

This is a tradition that has been maintained for many years and is part of the legend of the historic homestead of Kronendal in which the restaurant is housed. For more than 170 years reports have been published of Kronendal's ghost. The legend dates back to 1840 when the manor house was owned by the Cloete family.

The story goes that General Abraham Josias Cloete had a daughter, Elsa, who fell in love with a young soldier from the garrison in Hout Bay. However, her father forbade the match and the only contact the lovers had was through a top floor window, under the gable, where Elsa would stand and wave at her paramour across the street. The soldier is said to have hung himself in despair from a tree in the oak-lined avenue; Elsa died shortly afterwards of a broken heart.

Many unexplained incidents have been reported, including pots flying off hooks on the wall and lights dimming of their own accord. The apparition of a young woman has been seen on the staircase, or looking out of the window. A man has also been spotted standing among the oaks after sunset, looking up at the building. Since the 1970s there have been at least five sightings of Elsa's ghost reported in the local news.

Established in the late 17th century, Kronendal was the first farm in Hout Bay, although the front part of the homestead was built around 1800 by Johannes van Helsdingen. It's one of very few remaining H-shaped Cape Dutch houses on the peninsula and has a rare halsgewel gable with an elevated neck. It was declared a national monument in 1960.

MANGANESE JETTY

Mining on Constantiaberg

Manganese ore-loading jetty
Flora Bay, Hout Bay

When heading up Chapman's Peak Drive from Hout Bay, look to the sea below and you'll notice the remains of a concrete-and-steel jetty, usually dotted with cormorants drying themselves in the sun. These structures, 400 metres south of Hout Bay Beach, are the most visible reminders of Constantiaberg's old manganese mine.

The mine sits on the mountain slopes directly above the eastern end of Hout Bay Beach and was connected to the ore-loading jetty by a 700-metre-long chute. There was a collection point at the bottom where the ore was transferred by hand to coco-pans that ran on a light-rail track to the jetty. Here it was loaded into lighters for transfer to ships anchored in the bay. The ore was not processed at the Cape, but rather shipped to Europe where it was used either in the production of chlorine or as an alloying element with iron.

The presence of those resources at the Cape is first mentioned in 1676 when Jan van Riebeeck's son, Abraham, stopped here on his way to Batavia to inspect a site "near the Hout Bay." Manganese was the only mineral of economic importance ever mined in the bay. The deposits were ferruginous manganese ore (a combination of manganese and iron oxides).

Four sites are known to have been investigated in the area. Three of them were only prospects – sites investigated for the presence of the mineral but never commercially mined. The sites were at Bokkemanskloof (in the ravine above Oakhurst Farm), Constantia Nek (midway between the Nek and Constantiaberg) and Klein Koppie on the northwestern slope of Constantiaberg. Only the site known as Hout Bay Mine on the slopes above Flora Bay was actively worked.

The first recorded mining attempt was towards the end of the 19th century. A company was formed in 1880 to exploit the deposits, but this was short-lived. Successful mining seems to have begun in 1909 when it was reported that the difficulties of operating a mine in the area had been overcome and that manganese was being shipped to Belgium.

Production records are scant for the Hout Bay Manganese Company. But we do know that in January 1911, the mine produced some 130 tons. The company worked the area for a short period until May 1911 when it closed for good.

EAST FORT

An era when Hout Bay was of great strategic significance to the Cape

Hout Bay
The blockhouse ruins are on the mountain side of Chapman's Peak Drive, less than one kilometre south of Hout Bay Beach

Park your car at the blockhouse (above the road) and walk down to the battery of cannons and powder magazine below the road. This fort and blockhouse complex harks back to an era when Hout Bay was of great strategic significance to the Cape.

Early Dutch settlers realised that this sheltered bay could serve as an alternative anchorage when prevailing winds made Table Bay unsafe. The Dutch (and later British) administrations also realised that the bay offered a possible landing place for any invading military force.

Consequently, towards the end of the 18th century, the area saw the building of a number of fortifications: first at the foot of Hangberg and later on the eastern side of the bay below Chapman's Peak. Initial construction took place after 1775 when both France and Holland supported the newly-independent American colonies and declared war on England.

The garrison consisted of Khoikhoi troops quartered at Kronendal Farm, reinforced by a French Pondichery Regiment composed mainly of Indian sepoys under the command of Irish expatriate Count de Conway.

After the Royal Navy attacked a Dutch East India fleet at Saldanha Bay, a powerful battery was installed at East Fort with earthworks and large-calibre cannons. Some of the guns, with their VOC markings, are still in place and are fired on ceremonial occasions.

During the first British occupation of 1796, Royal Engineers constructed a fortified blockhouse. It was three storeys high, built of stone and had windows with wooden shutters. The ground floor housed a magazine and cisterns, while an exterior wooden stairway led up to the middle-floor command post and officers' quarters. Wooden galleries were affixed to the corners of the upper floor.

Large stone barracks for the troops were built higher up the mountain, as well as a guardhouse and sentry box at the entrance to the old road. You'll also notice the remains of a cookhouse opposite the blockhouse.

By 1804 the fortifications needed restoration. Although the new Batavian administration saw to their maintenance, by 1827 all the defences had been abandoned. The site was declared a national monument in 1936.

SECRET CAVE

Picnic at a geological contact point

Chapman's Peak Drive
30 metres below the main lookout point

There's a sheltered sandstone cave on Chapman's Peak Drive that boasts one of Cape Town's finest views. The cave lies just above an interesting 'contact line', easily distinguished by the different coloured rocks (ochre and red above, grey below).

Drive south out of Hout Bay, up Chapman's Peak until you reach the main lookout point at the summit of the drive. Park and walk to the end of the lookout point. Slip through the railings and follow a narrow path to the left that seems to disappear over the edge of the cliff.

There's enough space for a few groups to enjoy a picnic and take in the dreamy blues of sea and sky. Best of all is sundowners here: toasting the sun as it dips into the Atlantic beyond the Sentinel. Far below, you may spot whales, dolphins or fishing boats chugging out of Hout Bay harbour.

Chapman's Peak is one of the most dramatic drives in South Africa. The western flank of Constantiaberg falls steeply for hundreds of metres into the Atlantic. The road that hugs the near-vertical face of the mountain from Hout Bay to Noordhoek was hacked out of the face between 1915 and 1922. At the time, it was regarded as a supreme feat of engineering.

The upper part of Chapman's Peak consists of flat sedimentary rocks (younger than 520 million years old) related to the sandstone that forms Table Mountain. The base of the mountain, however, consists of Cape Granite (older than 540 million years) and the two formations meet at a geological unconformity that is world-famous among earth scientists.

Two different endangered vegetation types can be found along this road. The vegetation corresponds to the two main geological formations: Peninsula Sandstone Fynbos (above) and Cape Granite Fynbos (below), which are both endemic to Cape Town.

Chapman's Peak Drive

Chapman's Peak is named after John Chapman, the captain's mate of a Royal Navy ship that was becalmed in Hout Bay in 1607. The skipper sent his pilot, John Chapman, ashore in the hope of finding provisions. The pilot later recorded the bay as Chapman's Chaunce (chance) and the name stuck, becoming official on all East India charts.

In the early 1900s, Sir Nicolas Fredrick de Waal, first administrator of the Cape Province, ordered the construction of a road linking Hout Bay to Noordhoek. It was cleverly planned to follow the Cape Granite contour, while the many roadside cuttings could be carved out of the more workable sandstone sediments. The road took seven years to complete and was opened in 1922.

Southern Suburbs

THE FRENCH REDOUBT

The only remains of the French Line

Trafalgar Park, Searle Street, Woodstock

In a quiet park in Woodstock stand the remains of a series of fortifications hastily built by the French in 1781 to defend against British attack.

When the Dutch declared in favour of the American War of Independence in December of 1780, Britain used this as an excuse to declare war on the Netherlands and to seize the Cape, which they had long desired as a replenishment station. However, a spy in the British war office reported their plans to the French, who dispatched a fleet of ships to the Cape, carrying the Pondichery Regiment commanded by Colonel Conway.

On their arrival, the French assessed the Cape's fortifications and found them woefully inadequate. They found five points from which the Cape could be attacked: Table Bay, the neck between Table Mountain and Lion's Head, Hout Bay, False Bay and Saldanha Bay

To protect the settlement from a possible attack overland from False Bay, the Pondichery Regiment was deployed to construct a line of defences from Fort Knokke – where the Woodstock train station now stands – westwards across the farm of Zonnebloem to the foot of Devil's Peak. It consisted of four redoubts: Fort Knokke, the Hollandse Redoute, the Franse Redoute and the Burgher Redoute. This became known as the French Line, but was also referred to as the Zonnebloem, Munnik Line or the Nieuwe Retranchement. When the British fleet arrived, they decided the Cape of Good Hope was too strongly defended and attacked Saldanha Bay instead.

Five years after its construction, the French Line had fallen into such a state of disrepair that it was regarded as completely useless. But when the British fleet finally conquered the Cape in 1795, the redoubts were repaired along with the earthworks that connected them. The York, Prince of Wales, and King's Blockhouses on Devil's Peak were then added. The line remained in use until 1827 when orders were given to demolish all the forts except Fort Knokke. However, it was the Franse Redoute, also known as the Central, or Frederick William Redoubt, that was the only one to survive.

The redoubt has earth banks, a stone entrance and a conical chimney. It was traditionally assumed that this would have been an oven used to heat cannon balls before they were fired at wooden ships. However, research has shown that as the structure was only added in 1830, after the forts were decommissioned, it was probably a brick-kiln. The site was proclaimed a national monument in 1968.

ST GEORGE'S CATHEDRAL IN WOODSTOCK

Incandescent Greek Orthodox frescoes

75 Mountain Road, Woodstock
021-551-0788
For the times of church services: goarch.co.za

At the top of Cape Town's Adderley Street, St George's Cathedral (Anglican) is one of the best-known churches in South Africa. However, there's another, far less famous St George's Cathedral in the city.

The Greek cathedral (Agios Georgios) was built in 1903-04, just a few years after Cape Town received its first Greek Orthodox priest, and was expanded in 1983. It is of a neo-classical design, built for Cape Town's small Greek community. As cathedrals go, it's a humble building in a quiet corner of Woodstock. But nothing quite prepares you for the interior. Upon entering the building, you're immediately struck by the grandeur of the frescoes, icons, furnishings and ornamentation.

The walls, vaults and apse are all richly decorated with Byzantine-style frescoes depicting Jesus, the protecting saints and various icons. The frescoes were produced by Father Nikolai, a Romanian priest and hagiographer, who painted the interiors with two assistants in the 1990s under the guidance of Bishop Ioakim. Funding for the project was raised by subscription from members of the congregation.

The nave displays the Nativity, the life of the Virgin and the Agony of Christ, while the sanctuary is dominated by an image of Jesus sitting on the lap of the Virgin, presented as his protector. The vaults are rendered as a blue sky dotted with stars and Christ Pantocrator looks down from their midst.

As the early morning sun pours through the stained-glass windows, it illuminates the rich colours within. If you visit during a service, the chanting, white robes and incense transport you straight to the eastern Mediterranean. Look out for the archbishop's throne, flanked by a frieze depicting St Demetrios and St Minas.

The church was accorded cathedral status in 1968 and became the seat of the Ortho-dox Archbishopric of Good Hope, Patriarch of Alexandria and All Africa. The archdiocese presides over the Western, Northern and Eastern Cape provinces, the Orange Free State, Kwa-Zulu-Natal, Namibia, Lesotho and Swaziland.

THE TREATY TREE

The tree at which the Cape was handed to the British

Corner of Treaty and Spring Streets
Woodstock

Beside the railway tracks that run behind the furniture wholesale warehouses in Lower Woodstock is an old milkwood tree. The commemorative plaque on the rock beneath it was stolen some years ago, but it is nonetheless a national monument. It was here, on 10 January 1806, that the commandant of Cape Town, Lieutenant-Colonel Hieronymus Casimir von Prophalow, and the commanders of the British forces signed the treaty of the Battle of Blaauwberg. The treaty passed control of the Cape from Dutch to British hands, where it remained for more than a century, until it was incorporated into the Union of South Africa in 1910.

At the time of the treaty, the tree stood beside a homestead called Papendorp, after which the suburb of Woodstock was originally named. This building became known as Treaty House and the tree as the Treaty Tree. The house was demolished to make way for a factory in 1935, but the tree survived. In 1967 it was declared a national monument.

Although it's not certain how old the tree is, some say it was already a landmark for Portuguese sailors in the 16th century. Legend also has it that it was near this tree that 64 of cut-throat explorer Captain d'Almeida's infamous marines were massacred by local Khoikhoi in 1509 after foolishly attempting to abduct an infant from the clan.

Before 1806, the tree was known as the slave tree, as slaves were sold in its shade – and sometimes hanged from its branches. Until the end of the last century, there still lived in Woodstock a woman, Rachel Bester, who claimed to have seen the slave dealers touting their human wares under the tree.

It's interesting to note that, until the land reclamation of the Foreshore in 1952, the Treaty Tree would have been very close to the old Woodstock beach, with a fine view of the sea and ships coming in and out of the harbour.

This is probably the only tree in South Africa to have a wine named after it. The milkwood is pictured on the label of Flagstone's Treaty Tree Reserve – an award-winning blend of Sauvignon Blanc and Semillon.

The Milkwood

The milkwood (*Sideroxylon inerme*) is a low-growing, evergreen tree that can live for well over 1,000 years. In the past, its hard, strong wood was used for shipbuilding, bridges, mills and ploughs. The site of a farmyard was often determined by the presence of milkwoods. They are protected in South Africa; three other milkwood trees have been awarded national-monument status:

The Post Office Tree in Mossel Bay, Western Cape

Milkwood at Rhenosterfontein Farm, near Bredasdorp, Western Cape

The Fingo Milkwood Tree near Peddie, Eastern Cape

THE ORIGINAL NOON GUN

A small brass pistol

South African Astronomical Observatory, 1 Observatory Road, Observatory
Open nights every second and fourth Saturday of the month at 8pm
Free entry

TIME PISTOL AND POWDER FLASH

Time-keeping for the ships in port was a major responsibility for this Observatory at the beginning of the 19th Century. A few minutes before the arranged time, the Astronomer went on the roof of the main building with a chronometer and the brass-barrelled pistol displayed here. When the second hand of the chronometer reached the appointed time, the pistol was fired. At this point a signalman at the harbour watching through his telescope for the flash from the fired pistol, would drop a time ball by means of a rope attached to his foot. By taking note of this time signal, ships in port were able to set the chronometers, or time-keeping instruments, more accurately.

No one can fail to notice the boom that resounds through the City Bowl at noon every day, when the 'Noon Gun' is fired from Signal Hill. But even those who go to see the cannon are unaware that Cape Town's famous time signal was once sounded by a small brass pistol, now in a cabinet at the South African Astronomical Observatory (SAAO).

In 1820 the British Admiralty decided to set up a permanent observatory in the Cape to improve navigation and ensure the British Empire's naval dominance. Key to this was the provision of an accurate time service for ships. The first astronomer sent out by the Royal Astronomical Society, Fearon Fallows, arrived in 1821 with two portable instruments and a clock. He spent seven years battling to complete the observatory and had to signal the time from his house in Gardens using an oil lamp.

Fallows died in 1833 and was succeeded by Thomas Henderson, who started a new time service. Carrying a pocket chronometer and a brass percussion pistol loaded with black powder, Henderson would climb onto the observatory's roof and fire the gun at a specific time. Sailors with their telescopes aimed at the observatory would see the flash by night and the smoke by day, then set their chronometers accordingly.

Subsequent directors of the observatory introduced time balls, which were dropped at the observatory, on Signal Hill and at the docks. You can still see the time ball at the Waterfront. The electronic signal that fires the current noon gun still originates from the master clock of the SAAO, as it has been doing since 1864.

Henderson's signalling pistol is in a small museum in the McClean dome, which contains three functioning telescopes as well as one of Fallows' original portable instruments. Access is only on open nights, which include a 45-minute talk, a tour of the site and stargazing.

A Constellation Named After Table Mountain

One of the first astronomers at the Cape was Abbé Nicolas-Louis de la Caille, who charted almost 10,000 southern stars between 1751 and 1753. These included a faint constellation near the Southern Cross containing part of the Large Magellanic Cloud. Its resemblance to Table Mountain's famous tablecloth inspired De la Caille to call it 'Mons Mensa' – the only constellation named after a geographical feature on earth.

BULI STOOL

A chief's stool from Africa's heart

Irma Stern Museum
Cecil Road, Rosebank
021-685-5686
irmastern.co.za
Tuesday–Friday 10am–5pm; Saturday 10am–2pm

The Irma Stern Museum occupies the original home of this famous South African artist (1894-1966). Apart from her paintings, the museum is full of artefacts that Stern collected on her numerous trips to Europe and into Africa. Although she travelled to the Congo three times in the 1940s and 50s, it is thought that the Buli stool was acquired either in Europe in the 1920s or on a trip to Zanzibar in 1939.

The Luba chief's stool, or Buli stool, is the jewel of Stern's collection. Similar examples can be found in the Metropolitan Museum of Art in New York and the British Museum. This stool is one of only 20 known items attributed to the atelier of the Master of Buli, a village in Katanga Province, south-eastern Democratic Republic of Congo. Whether the work is by the master himself or by apprentices is unclear.

This style of carving is characterised by elongated faces, which suggest age and stature. The stools were not meant as seats but rather represented the chief and his people's connection with the spirit world. This particular caryatid figure is thought to show a female ancestor symbolically supporting the chief. The hairstyle and body scarification suggest high social status. The depiction of a female figure supporting a male chief alludes to the Luba system of matrilineal descent in which a man's political position is inherited from his mother.

The stool sits in a glass cabinet and is the centrepiece of the museum's Congo Room. Turquoise walls have been hung with gouaches and oils produced by the artist during her Congo journeys or painted later in her Rosebank studio from sketches. These works include portraits of the Mangbetu people, landscapes, markets and dancing scenes.

The Irma Stern Museum was established in 1971 in the house in which the artist lived for almost four decades. Several of the rooms are still furnished as she left them, while upstairs there's a commercial gallery used by contemporary artists.

The permanent collection on display shows Irma Stern's development as an artist. Subject matter ranges from exotic figures and portraits to landscapes and still lifes produced in a variety of media, including oil, watercolour, gouache and charcoal.

> *"The Congo has always been for me the symbol of Africa, the very heart of Africa."* Irma Stern

WELGELEGEN MANOR HOUSE

A Herbert Baker classic

Chapel Road Extension in Rosebank ends in the grounds of Welgelegen
The house is closed to the public but the university runs occasional tours
021-650-3759

Welgelegen Manor House lies in the Middle Campus of the University of Cape Town and accommodates the Communication and Marketing Department. It is a fine building, with asymmetrical gables, and sits in a spectacular spot on the slopes of Devil's Peak. As it is an administrative building, the interiors are generally not open to the public.

Welgelegen was designed by the Cape's most famous architect, Herbert Baker, in the grounds of Groote Schuur Estate in 1899. It is a fine example of Baker's Cape Dutch Revival Style – a happy blend of Cape Dutch and English country-house fashions. Welgelegen used to have elegant Arts and Crafts interiors which included a dining table designed by Baker himself. Unfortunately, the house was gutted by the new owners. If you want to get a sense of the original décor, pop into the house and ask to see the three paintings by James Durden depicting the interiors.

The property dates back to the 17th century. In 1657 the VOC (Dutch East India Company) granted land on the slopes of Table Mountain to a number of free burghers under the leadership of Steven Bothma, who established the farm Welgelegen. After his death, the estate changed hands a number of times until 1756, when it became the property of Jacob van Reenen.

The original house was erected in the 18th century and substantially altered by Baker. Commissioned by Cecil John Rhodes, the mining magnate gave Welgelegen to John Blades Currey, a friend who'd been good to him during his early Kimberley days when the young empire-builder was taken ill. Currey was the manager of a Northern Cape land-owning company (later absorbed into De Beers Consolidated Mines with Rhodes as chairman) and was responsible for giving Kimberley its name when he was serving as government secretary there. Back in Cape Town, Currey was made steward of Rhodes's vast estate, Groote Schuur. Welgelegen remained a Currey home from 1900 to 1979, when the university procured the house after the death of Currey's daughter, Winifred. It was declared a national monument in 1980.

"Nature's handiwork is on a larger scale ... in South Africa which the Arch-Architect has designed so essentially in the grand manner."
Herbert Baker

THE OLD ZOO REMAINS

Until 1978 real lions lived here

Groote Schuur Estate, near the corner of Madiba Circle and Rhodes Memorial Street
Rondebosch

On the slopes of Table Mountain, beside the Upper Campus of the University of Cape Town, are the remains of the old Groote Schuur Zoo and the stone enclosure that was once the lions' den.

Originally built by Cecil John Rhodes, who bought vast tracts of land on Table Mountain in the 1890s, the zoo was situated above his former residence at Groote Schuur, now the Cape Town residence of the South African president. Rhodes wanted to create a menagerie of animals from all over the British Empire for the public to enjoy.

At first the menagerie contained only herbivorous species housed in large paddocks. But in 1897, when Rhodes was given a pair of lions and a leopard, a special enclosure was built for them.

Rhodes had his architect, Sir Herbert Baker, draw up plans for a noble, colonnaded lion house. Ultimately, a smaller cage was constructed. The zoo was designed to tell an evolutionary story, presenting animals in ascending order of superiority: reptiles at the bottom, birds and monkeys in the middle and lions, as 'King of the Beasts', at the top.

Upon Rhodes's death in 1902, he bequeathed his estate to the nation and specified that the zoo be kept open to the public free of charge. In 1931 the original lion cages were torn down and a new enclosure built.

The Groote Schuur Zoo opened every day at 9am and closed again at 5pm to the sound of a whistle. The lions were fed on donkeys and horses kept in an enclosure behind the den. People living in the nearby suburbs of Rondebosch and Newlands could hear the lions roaring for food if a westerly wind was blowing.

In 1978 the zoo was closed due to growing concerns about animal welfare as well as the expense of running it. Since then it has been used as informal housing, an art exhibition space and even a theatre and restaurant.

A giraffe sent from the Transvaal has its neck broken

There's no record of exactly which animals were kept in the zoo, but many were added and removed over the years: a lion cub was exchanged for a camel from a circus; a kangaroo that escaped was caught in a leopard trap and shot by a farmer; and a giraffe, sent from the Transvaal by train, never arrived because railway officers put it in an open truck and its neck was broken when the train entered a tunnel.

GROOTE SCHUUR RESIDENCE

The grandest of Cecil John Rhodes's residences

Klipper Road, Rondebosch
083-414-7961
Tours by appointment only

Although Cecil John Rhodes liked to open his gardens at Groote Schuur to the public every weekend, visitors are not exactly encouraged these days. The estate is now the official residence of South Africa's president. Security is tight and tours must be arranged in advance and a passport or identity document provided.

Nonetheless, a visit is well worth the effort. Set against the slopes of Table Mountain, this magnificent house was first built as a granary in 1658 by the Dutch East India Company, accounting for its name, which means 'Great Barn'. After Cecil John Rhodes became Prime Minister of the Cape Colony in 1890, he first rented the property and then purchased it in 1893. He then commissioned a young, unknown British architect visiting Cape Town to renovate the building. It was Herbert Baker's first project in South Africa and led to his creation of what became known as the Cape Dutch Revival Style.

After a suspicious fire destroyed a portion of the house in December 1896, Baker and Rhodes reconstructed and modernised the building using handmade ironmongery and antique Dutch and Spanish tiles, bricks and lanterns. Rhodes commissioned agents to find original furniture, silver and glassware from the Cape, some of which had to be re-imported from Holland. Where no suitable furniture could be found, Baker designed pieces himself.

Rhodes bequeathed his estate to the nation and from 1911 until 1994 Groote Schuur was the official Cape residence of South Africa's prime ministers and presidents. It was here in 1990 that FW de Klerk and Nelson Mandela signed the 'Groote Schuur Minute', an historic commitment to peaceful negotiations.

The teak-lined manor is now a museum, housing a fine collection of Delft ceramics, Chinese and Japanese porcelain, 17th-century Flemish tapestries and many other treasures, including Rhodes's personal library and one of only three Dolmetsch 'Beethoven' fortepianos ever made, which visitors are sometimes invited to play.

A Unique Piece of Zimbabwe's Cultural Heritage

Possibly one of the most significant but overlooked treasures is to be found in Rhodes's old bedroom, which has been kept exactly as he left it. On top of a glass-fronted cabinet is one of the original carved soapstone birds from the ruins of Great Zimbabwe, one the most important civilisations in Africa. It is the only one of the five birds stolen from the site that has not yet been returned and it comes as something of a shock to anyone familiar with Great Zimbabwe that this unique piece of Zimbabwe's cultural heritage remains here, apparently unnoticed.

THE RONDEBOSCH FOUNTAIN

*A lamp post which used to be an ornamental
drinking trough for drivers, draught horses and dogs*

Intersection of Main and Belmont Roads, Rondebosch

The lamp post at the intersection of Main and Belmont Roads is not your usual lamp post – it used to be an ornamental drinking trough for drivers, draught horses, and dogs. Note the attention to detail with the legs of the fountain in the shape of horse hooves, and the lower drinking troughs for dogs placed between them. Today, plants occupy the horse drinking trough and are watered by a local resident.

Unveiled in September 2020, the Rondebosch ornamental fountain, as it is officially called, is a replica of the original Rondebosch Fountain that was destroyed in August 2015 by a drunk driver.

A gift from Mr George Pigot-Moodie (residing close by at Westbrook, known today as Genadendal, the residence of the President of South Africa), the original iconic monument was inaugurated on 26 September 1891. Affectionately referred to as the Moodie Fountain, six months later it became the first electric streetlight: the circuit was initially supplied by the then late Moodie's private plant until the generating plant in Rondebosch became available. The fountain was declared a National Monument in 1964.

Born in Grahamstown in 1829, Moodie was a surveyor and railway pioneer who wanted to give back to his community. The original fountain was cast in Glasgow by Walter Macfarlane & Co Ltd (1872–1967) in their Saracen Foundry. Their exclusive agent in South Africa was the architect Charles Freeman, who had a catalogue offering a vast range of cast iron products for his clients in South Africa. Drinking fountains were not manufactured from a single mould – several castings would have been prepared so that they could be shipped the long distance. In addition, this concept offered clients a sense of customisation.

It was local resident and owner of Heritage Castings Max Teichman who undertook the project of creating a new replica in 2020. It was lucky that the skilled veteran artist Stephen Wood (now in his 80s) was available to spend over 200 hours hand-crafting the wooden moulds to recreate the intricate details of the original fountain. While cast iron was typical for the 19th century, today it is known to be unsuitable, and therefore cast aluminium was used for the new fountain. With the original foundry no longer in existence and no available records, archival photographs were researched to ensure the accuracy of this new fountain.

JOSEPHINE MILL

The city's last working waterwheel

13 Boundary Road
Newlands
Monday–Fridag 9am–1pm

Josephine Mill (1840) is Cape Town's only surviving operational watermill and forms part of a museum dedicated to the milling industry. Power was generated by an iron waterwheel that was attached to the elegant Victorian structure set on a leafy street beside the Newlands rugby stadium. The brick building, with its cast-iron windows, is reminiscent of similar architecture in Sweden, home of the first owner, Jacob Letterstedt.

Josephine Mill was bequeathed to the Cape Town Historical Society by its heir, Myra East, in 1975. At the time, the structure was in a state of considerable disrepair. Abandoned in the 1930s, parts of the building had been exposed to the elements for decades, but a few records hinting at its construction and workings inspired the society to renovate.

Upon clearing the building and the surroundings of debris, much of the mill's defunct machinery was unearthed. From these relics and a few records, the society restored the building to full operation. A major challenge was to recreate the original watercourses to supply the waterwheel and harness the power of the Liesbeek River. By 1988, the iron wheel was turning once more, able to produce freshly milled, stone-ground flour.

The museum's interior houses artefacts recovered from the area and an exhibition of the stone-milling process. There are plans showing the original watercourses and pipes, along with a Cornish steam boiler that was found on the banks of the Liesbeek. Also on display are French Burr milling stones. These are not cut from one piece but rather built up from sections of quartz, cemented together with plaster, dressed with a pattern to assist with grinding and bound with iron bands. French Burr comes from the Marne Valley in northern France.

The mill has an interesting history. Jacob Letterstedt, a young immigrant from Sweden, took a job as manager of a farm on the banks of the Liesbeek River. He eventually married the owner, a wealthy widow 18 years his senior. Letterstedt built the mill in 1840 and imported the waterwheel from England. It was a precisely engineered machine with 10 horsepower.

Letterstedt named the mill in honour of Crown Princess Josephine of Sweden. He also built an elegant, five-storey steam mill with a tall, decorative chimney adjoining Josephine Mill.

NEWLANDS SPRING

The source of the Cape's brewing industry

Springs Way, Newlands
Water collection point: corner of Letterstedt and Main Roads
Daily 6am–9pm
Free entry

A t the end of a quiet cul-de-sac in an old part of Newlands, a white plastic pipe juts from the ground. Out of it burbles clear, cool spring water. This is the overflow from Newlands Spring, which is situated under the ground just here. It may not seem much to look at, but this water was a key factor in the development of the suburb and was pivotal to the history of brewing in South Africa.

Newlands Spring is actually one of several in the area; the early Newlands settlements and estates relied on these springs for domestic and industrial use. The first brewery license granted in South Africa was in Newlands in 1694 and by the late 1880s four breweries had been established in the area: Hiddingh's Cannon Brewery, Letterstedt's Mariendahl Brewery, Cloete's Newlands Brewery and Ohlsson's Annenberg Brewery. They all used water from the Newlands Spring, considered the finest quality water for the best beer in the Cape.

Anders Ohlsson eventually acquired the other breweries, along with their water rights to the Newlands Spring, to become Ohlsson's Cape Breweries. However, the land and the spring now belong to South African Breweries (SAB). This is somewhat ironic as SAB grew out of the Johannesburg-based Castle Breweries. Back in the early 1900s, it was Castle Lager that became the fiercest competitor of Ohlsson's Lion Lager.

The spring still provides more than 1.5 million litres of water to the Newlands Brewery each day – a volume that has been consistent since a pipe was installed from the spring to the brewery in 1942. Before then, the spring water was led to the brewery by an open channel. The spring water is tested regularly, and is of very high quality. It has a pH of 5.9 (the more acidic water is, the more hydrogen it contains and the more hydrating it is). It has a low mineral content and no contaminants.

SAB have set up a convenient collection point on the corner of Letterstedt and Main Roads, which is open to the public daily between 6am and 9pm. On any given day, a steady trickle of people arrives to collect water. From men in suits and BMWs to car guards from the parking lot across the road, policemen and hippies, housewives and pensioners, carrying every type of water container you can imagine. The spring is a unifying force and a joyful secret shared by these Capetonians.

PARADISE

The remains of the first master woodcutter's cottage

Newlands Forest, Union Avenue, Newlands
Take the Newlands Forest turnoff from the M3, where you will immediately see a parking area. Walk up the tar road, turn left and continue. Take the third turn to the left (each turn is marked with a bench), keep right and you will find Paradise
Sunrise to sunset, year round
Free entry

Among red alders, white stinkwoods and English oaks, deep in Newlands Forest, lie the ruins of a stone cottage known as 'Paradise'. Although the ruins date back to the mid-1700s, the first person to inhabit the site arrived in 1657, just five years after Van Riebeeck.

Leenderts Cornelis, a free carpenter and sawyer, was granted the use of 'Het Paradijs' and a stretch of forest including what is now Newlands and Kirstenbosch. His task was to protect the forest from indiscriminate hacking and to provide a steady supply of wood for the settlement. But in 1661 he was discharged for brawling and swearing.

By 1714, the forests of Table Mountain were so depleted that the Company had to apply firm controls. A master woodcutter and a garrison of soldiers were sent to Paradise to patrol the forest for illegal woodcutters (though they often caught runaway slaves and bandits instead).

The first permanent buildings were erected in 1735, but a more 'luxurious' house – the ruins of which you can see today – was built between 1750 and 1770. A little way from the main house are the remains of the garrison accommodation; further on is an outhouse, thought to have been a stable. While the woodcutter and his family enjoyed relative comfort, the soldiers survived on poor pay, poor rations and brutal discipline. They were even known to steal vegetables from surrounding farms in desperation. It's unlikely that this was the life they'd envisaged when they enlisted in Amsterdam to escape Europe's economic depression!

The walls of Paradise are a combination of stone and brick – some local, and some imported Dutch 'klinkers'. The stone foundations limited damp and created a base for the heavy timber and thatch roof. The gable was built entirely of stone to withstand the southeasterly wind; in it you can still see slots for the roof beams.

From 1797 until 1800, Lady Anne Barnard and her husband Andrew used the house as a country getaway. Thanks to Lady Anne's famous diaries, Paradise is also known, perhaps inappropriately, as 'Lady Anne Barnard's Cottage'. Today, only the low stone walls and gable remain as evidence of the pioneers that once inhabited the house: an outpost consumed by the forest it was established to protect.

THE BOSHOF GATEWAY

One of the finest old Cape gateways

Intersection of Paradise Road and Boshof Avenue, Newlands

Every day, busy Capetonians whizz past an elegant whitewashed wooden gateway that stands just off the busy M3 motorway in Newlands. It's unlikely that many of these motorists know about, or even notice, the original entrance to the old Boshof Estate, which dates back to the 18th century.

From 1658, the land from Mowbray to Newlands was divided into a patchwork of estates bordering the Liesbeek River. In 1666, the space that lay in a fork formed by the old wagon road to the forest and the main road to the south was granted to the miller Wouter Mostert (not the same Mostert the mill was named after). Mostert called his farm Goed en Quaad, meaning 'Good and Evil'. It was later consolidated with a small adjacent farm (Boshof) and was described as being "in the wilderness, to the north of the Liesbeek River." It probably extended from the mountain to the river and from the gateway to where Kirstenbosch is now.

Alexander van Breda took possession of the farm in 1786 and apparently erected the gateway very soon afterwards. It seems likely that it is the work of Cape Malay slaves, many of whom were skilled artisans

and craftsmen. It was designed in a neo-classical style, with urns and magnificently profiled heads. Today it is regarded as one of the finest and best-preserved old Cape gateways. It opens onto Boshof Avenue, one of the oldest avenues in the Cape, where the gable of the original Boshof House, dated 1776, can be seen from the sidewalk.

The Boshof Gateway was declared a national monument in 1941.

Estates that became suburbs

Travelling south from Cape Town, the first estate was Welgelegen (see page 132), which was adjoined by Zorgvliet, of which nothing – not even a street name – remains. The next farm, Rustenberg, was the governors' residence until 1791. Groote Schuur, also initially government-owned, was the neighbouring farm, followed by Klein Schuur. Above and to the south-west was Mount Pleasant, below which lay Westervoot, later anglicised as Westerford. Papenboom, also known as the Brouwery, was where the first Cape beer was brewed in 1696. Newlands, originally Nieuwland, became the governors' country residence in the late 1700s. South of Newlands were Boshof, Fernwood and Paradijs, an old Company farm. Van Riebeeck's farm, Boschheuvel, lay in the valley beyond, and is now Bishopscourt.

THE HERSCHEL OBELISK

A tribute to a distinguished astronomer

Grove Primary School, Grove Avenue, Claremont

In the middle of a small school in Claremont is a monument to Sir John FW Herschel, the famous British astronomer and only son of the equally famous astronomer Sir William Herschel.

Herschel arrived at the Cape in 1834 to make observations of the southern skies. He brought with him a six-metre reflecting telescope, which he mounted in the garden of Feldhausen Estate, where he lived until 1838. During his stay, he charted the Argo Nebula, catalogued objects in the Magellanic Clouds and located nearly 2,000 other nebulae and star clusters. He also discovered more than 1,200 pairs of double stars and observed Halley's Comet when it made its appearance between 1835 and 1836. In addition to his astronomical work, Herschel helped lay the building blocks for the education system in the Cape, emphasising maths and science.

When Herschel left, he sold Feldhausen with the condition that a 20-metre circular patch of ground where his telescope had stood would remain his property in perpetuity. At its centre Herschel placed a small granite column marked with his initials and the dates of his stay. Subsequently, members of the South African Literary and Scientific Institution, of which he had been president, decided to commemorate his scientific achievements and contributions to education in the Cape with 'a permanent memorial'.

A yellow granite column of Craigleith stone from a quarry near Edinburgh, costing about 300 pounds sterling, was erected in 1841 over Herschel's own column. You can see it from one side of the base of the obelisk, which has been left open. This space also originally contained a time capsule with six gold medallions, a map of the colony, Maclear's triangulation of Cape Town, engravings of nebulae and comets, statistical reports, a scale and coins. Inscriptions in English, Dutch and Latin were added to the other three sides.

The Latin inscription can be translated as follows:

"At this site John FW Herschel placed a very large mirror that he made with his own hands in England and for four years he expertly observed the furthest extent to which stars and nebulae in the sky shine, their position and their types. Thus the son dutifully completed in Africa as if by the same eye the outstanding work begun by his famous father and by himself in the northern hemisphere."

The obelisk was among the first national monuments proclaimed in 1936.

CHAMPION TREES
AT THE ARDERNE GARDENS

The largest collection of remarkable trees in South Africa

222 Main Road, Claremont
Daily 8am–6pm
Free entry / Donation box
A map of its noteworthy trees can be bought from the Scala pharmacy across the street

A small botanical garden in the heart of Claremont features six of South Africa's most remarkable trees. When the Department of Water Affairs and Forestry introduced a law in 2003 protecting designated 'Champion Trees' (i.e. trees of exceptional importance and heritage value), the Arderne Gardens turned out to have the largest single collection of trees worthy of protection.

Most impressive, perhaps, is a 37-metre (120-foot) tall Moreton Bay fig. With its sinuous spreading roots, it's one of the largest trees in South Africa and is affectionately known as the Wedding Tree, as many generations of Capetonians have had their wedding photographs taken with it. An Aleppo pine, towering to a height of 40 metres (130 feet) is double the usual height for the species and thought to be the largest of its kind in the world. And a 43-metre (140 foot) high Norfolk Island pine is the ancestor of the first Norfolk Island pine in South Africa. Bought for the princely sum of £5, the original tree was planted at the centre of the gardens in 1847, but died in 1914. It is possible that all Norfolk Island pines in South Africa trace their origin to it. The three other designated champion trees – an ancient Turkey oak, a wizened cork oak, and a Queensland kauri – are possibly less spectacular, though no less beautiful.

Most of the trees were planted by the gardens' creator, Ralph Henry Arderne, a timber merchant who bought the land (originally part of the old Stellenberg Estate) in 1845. Using his connections in the timber trade, Arderne was able to gratify his love of exotic trees and plants, amassing one of the finest collections in South Africa. An amble around the gardens will take you past a monstrous dragon tree from the Canary Islands, Australian bunya bunyas with 5kg cones, giant tree ferns from New Zealand, parana pines from Brazil, Himalayan deodars from India, Californian redwoods and probably the only Rule araucaria from New Caledonia in South Africa. After his death, Arderne's equally passionate son Henry continued to add to the collection, most notably with the rare flowering *Watsonia borbonica Ardernii* – which was named after him when he discovered it on a hike in the Cederberg.

The gardens are now a national monument, maintained by the City of Cape Town and the Friends of the Arderne Gardens.

STELLENBERG GARDENS

The most beautiful private garden in the Cape

30 Oak Avenue, Kenilworth
021-761-2948
Tuesday, Wednesday and Friday, by appointment only on 10am-1pm and
2pm–4.30pm with 3pm being the last tour booking of the day

Tucked away in the upmarket suburb of upper Kenilworth is a house that has been described by historians as the most beautiful in the Cape Peninsula. However, it is the gardens of Stellenberg that have received even greater acclaim of late. In the late 1980s, the current owners of Stellenberg, Sandy and Andrew Ovenstone, began the process of transforming the old gardens, with their ancient oaks, wide lawns, huge poplars and wild undergrowth, into something as unique and beautiful as the house they surround.

Once or twice a year, the Ovenstones open Stellenberg's gardens to the public. For a small fee – which goes to charity – you can roam the grounds at leisure, delighting in a series of outdoor 'rooms'. For this is how the gardens have been planned: there are 12 distinct areas, designed by using the old walls and the grounds' topography to structure the gardens as a series of inter-leading rooms. Each garden has a different theme and mood, but all aim to create a sense of peace and serenity.

After Sandy Ovenstone first arrived at Stellenberg in 1973, she nurtured a growing passion for gardening by touring famous English gardens, such as Sissinghurst and Hidcote, as well as local gardens, such as Babylonstoren. In 1987, with the help of interior designers Graham Viney and Gary Searle, she finally created her first garden at Stellenberg: the Herb Garden, in the shape of a St Andrew's cross.

A couple of years later, renowned English interior and garden designer David Hicks helped her convert the tennis court into the Walled Garden. This was originally planted with roses, although later, as Sandy Ovenstone became interested in more contemporary gardening trends, it was reworked to showcase spectacular perennials enclosed in borders of clipped myrtle.

South African garden designer Franchesca Watson played an important role in the design of the Medieval Garden – with its fountain of Paarl granite and combination of organic fruit, vegetables and medicinal herbs – and the Garden of Reflection, which features three black pools that reflect the sky, enclosed by towering hedges. Watson's work can also be seen in the Stream Garden, a tribute to the water source that would have been an important factor in the founding of the original farm in the 1700s.

Other gardens include the Wild Garden, a shady jungle featuring indigenous African plants; the Pool Garden, with borders of blue- and purple-flowering plants enhancing the pool's turquoise colour; and the White Garden, blooming with scented white flowers of all kinds.

KENILWORTH RACECOURSE CONSERVATION AREA

The best protected example of this unique ecosystem on the Cape Peninsula

Kenilworth Racecourse, Rosmead Avenue, Kenilworth
Contact KRCA viakrca.co.za
Entrance only by prior arrangement, on organised walks
The friends of the KRCA arrange flower walks in spring, frog walks in August, and even occasional spider walks
Fees for walks are usually R10-R20

Few people would associate horse racing with nature conservation. For most Capetonians, South Africa's oldest racecourse is best known as the home of the annual J&B Met, a prestigious racing and fashion event. Yet the veld that's been encircled by the lush green track since 1882 has also been inadvertently protected by it.

The 52 hectares of Cape Flats sand fynbos at the centre of the course have not been disturbed for more than 130 years, making this the best protected example of the ecosystem on the Cape Peninsula. Although the area was identified as one of 35 core botanical sites in the country back in 1882, formal conservation only started in 2006.

What appears from a distance to be ordinary scrub is, in fact, home to more than 350 indigenous plant species, 34 of which are endangered and two of which (*Erica margaritacea* and *Isolepis bulbifera*) are found nowhere else on earth. It's been suggested that no other single urban, natural-vegetation remnant comes close in terms of plant species numbers relative to physical area.

Two ericas classified as extinct in the wild, *Erica verticillata* and *Erica turgida*, were reintroduced after a controlled ecological burn in March 2005 and are now flourishing. Sectional burns performed every year since 2010 have led to the rediscovery of the cinnamon sambreëltjie (*Hessea cinnamomea*), which hadn't flowered there for more than 70 years.

Within the conservation area are several seasonal wetlands, which are breeding grounds for nine different frog species. These include one of only four remaining populations of the critically endangered Cape Flats frog or micro frog (*Microbatrachella capensis*), which is endemic to the southwestern Cape. Measuring just 15mm when fully grown, the micro frog is one of the smallest amphibians in South Africa. Breeding starts in the rainy winter season, usually between July and September, which is the best time to see and hear them. During the dry summer months, the micro frogs bury themselves in the thick grasses lining the wetlands and go into aestivation – a dormant state similar to hibernation – to avoid desiccation.

Also present in the reserve are 21 reptile species, including the tiny parrot-beaked tortoise, which grows to only 10cm in length. About 90 bird species live in or visit the reserve, one of which is the rare peregrine falcon.

WYNBERG MILITARY AQUATIC CENTRE

18

A heated pool on a military base open to the public

Corner of Scoble and Buren Roads, Wynberg Military Base, Wynberg
Daily 10am–3pm

I f your favourite exercise is swimming, but you're not a member of a gym, your options are very slim in Cape Town during winter. The only public pool that stays open is the Long Street Baths. However, although the Long Street pool is heated, it can become somewhat crowded and it isn't always entirely clean. Fortunately, there's another swimming pool suitable for training. It doesn't require a membership and hardly anyone in Cape Town has heard of it.

The Wynberg Military Aquatic Centre can be difficult to find, even when you know it's there, so be sure to use a GPS, as the residents of the military base may not be able to help you with accurate directions. The centre is run by a school called Swimlab, but casual swimmers are welcome. The covered 25-metre pool has four lanes and is kept heated to 24ºC. When we visited, the only other swimmer was Darren Murray, a South African Olympic backstroke swimmer. There are basic change-room and shower facilities and there is a grassy area around the pool, but it's more of a training facility than a family recreation spot.

Visiting the swimming pool also offers an excuse to explore the Wynberg Military Base, which is, with the exception of the Castle, the oldest military establishment in South Africa. The base dates back to 1797, but most of the original buildings have been demolished. However, the Victorian-style officer's mess, built in 1888 and declared a national monument in 1969, can still be seen.

Another Public Pool with a View

Although it's only open between mid-October and March, the Trafalgar Park public swimming pool just off Searle Street in Woodstock is the other best-kept-secret swimming spot in Cape Town. The 48-metre pool is just shy of Olympic size and has fantastic views of Devil's Peak and Table Mountain. It's surrounded by a pleasant grassy park with palm trees and a kiddies' paddling pool. On particularly hot weekends and during school holidays, the shallow end may fill up with local children. But during the week, the chances are it'll be just you, the lifeguard, and a cheeky seagull or two. It's open daily 10am-5pm.

THE SINGULAR CYCAD

19

The loneliest plant in the world

Kirstenbosch National Botanical Gardens
Daily 8am–6pm

What has been called 'the loneliest plant in the world' stands among a host of its relatives in the cycad dell at Kirstenbosch. *Encephalartos woodii*, or Wood's cycad, was discovered in the oNgoye Forest in KwaZulu-Natal by John Medley Wood in 1895. Wood, who was the curator of the Durban Botanic Gardens, found one clump of four trunks, all part of the same plant. The cycad was identified as a new species and named after him in 1908.

In 1903 Wood sent his deputy James Wylie to collect some of the smaller offshoots. In 1907 Wylie returned to collect two of the larger trunks, which still grow in the Durban Botanic Gardens. By 1912 there was only one three-metre tall trunk left in the wild. This was sent to the Government Botanist in Pretoria in 1916, but died in 1964. Despite numerous excursions to the forest since, no others have been found. The plant is now considered extinct in the wild.

What makes this a problem for *E woodii* is that cycads are dioecious – there are separate male and female plants. The plant that Wood stumbled on was male; no female seems to exist. This tall, palm-like plant, with a lineage going back about 340 million years, predates the dinosaurs and somehow survived through five ice ages, yet now appears unable to procreate.

All specimens of *E woodii* were grown from suckers of the original plant. It's one of the rarest and most highly prized plants in the world, with suckers selling for as much as $20,000. A sucker sold by Kirstenbosch fetched R89,000 (about $7,500), which was considered a bargain. You'll notice that the tree at Kirstenbosch is surrounded by a cage to prevent theft of the suckers.

Although there's still hope that another wild (*hopefully female*) specimen may one day be found somewhere in the oNgoye Forest, botanists are trying different techniques to create a female *E woodii*. One method is using pollen from its cones to fertilise its closest relative, *Encephalartos natalensis*, then crossing the offspring with *E woodii* again over many generations. However, this is a slow process and the hybrids would never be 'pure' *E woodii*. Other scientists are hoping that one of the male plants will undergo a spontaneous sex change – something that's been known to happen in other cycads.

Until then, as biologist Richard Fortey wrote, "this is the most solitary organism in the world, growing older, alone, and fated to have no successors."

VAN RIEBEECK'S HEDGE

Arboreal evidence of apartheid's earliest manifestation

Kirstenbosch National Botanical Gardens
Daily 8am–6pm

Concealed within the 'magic forest' section of Kirstenbosch Botanical Gardens are several huge and ancient wild-almond trees. Although they create pleasant shade for picnics and fabulous jungle gyms for children, their origin is somewhat less blithe.

The largest of these trees predate the gardens by more than two centuries. They are the remains of a hedge planted by Jan van Riebeeck's men in 1660, just a few years after the Dutch East India Company (VOC) established their outpost at the Cape. Whether by accident or design, the new settlement lay in the path of the local Khoikhoi people's traditional grazing routes. Naturally, this resulted in ongoing conflict between the groups, as well as stock theft.

The Dutch administration decided to enclose 'their' land by planting "bitter almonds and all kinds of quick-growing thorn bushes in the form of a land barrier so thick that no cattle or sheep will be able to be driven through it." Although building such boundaries was apparently common practice in Holland, it proved to be an eerie forerunner of the outlook that led to the development of apartheid, with white colonists seizing choice land and forcibly excluding the native Africans.

Ironically, although the hedge grew thick and fast, it proved an inconvenience to its own creators. The best grazing turned out to be on the other side and the settlement grew so rapidly that the Dutch soon needed to pasture their cattle outside the boundary in any case.

The portion of Van Riebeeck's hedge that remains in Kirstenbosch is older than any existing man-made structure from that time – including the Castle – and was among the first national monuments formally declared in South Africa on 17 April 1936. Interestingly, the Afrikaans words for fence and hedge are identical, although there are different words for each in Dutch.

The Wild Almond

Although it is colloquially known as the 'bitteramandel' and 'wild almond', *Brabejum stellatifolium* is not an almond at all, but a member of the protea family. Strangely, its closest botanical relatives are not in South Africa, but in far off Australia and the South Pacific. The fruits are poisonous, and caused South Africa's first recorded human death by poisoning when a man died in 1655 from eating too many bitter 'amandelen'. However, wild almonds formed an important food source for the Khoikhoi, who rendered them edible by soaking, boiling and roasting them.

THE ENDEMIC PROJECT

A secret night-time nature tour

Rhodes Drive
Constantia

Driving towards Hout Bay at night, on the forest road between Kirstenbosch Botanical Gardens and the Constantia Nek traffic circle, you'll notice a strange phenomenon. Along the side of this dark road, which is unlit by any street lamps, your headlights will pick up a cryptic sign that simply says, "once upon a time", followed by a procession of glowing creatures: butterflies, frogs, sunbirds, antelope and tortoises.

They are all part of an immersive installation experience by local filmmaker and artist Bryan Little. Tired of creating conventional videos, Little wanted to experiment with the traditional film experience and find a new way of telling stories. The Endemic Project is one of his first attempts at what he calls 'future film'. He decided to remove the camera and place the audience inside the scene, making the car's motion the element of time and narrative. Little says he wanted to "turn people's cars into spaceships to take them on a journey to explore their back garden."

Made from reflector tape on dark backgrounds, the 'light paintings' depict species of plants and animals endemic to the Western Cape that are no longer found in this suburb. The soundtrack was created by

sound designer Simon Kohle and uses atmospheric music accompanied by the sounds of the animals. When you take the tour, watch out for the geometric tortoise, the Table Mountain ghost frog and the orange-breasted sunbird.

Experiencing the Project

You'll need a smartphone that has GPS enabled. Install the free 'VoiceMap: Audio Walking Tours' app from the iTunes Store or Google Play. Look for 'The Endemic Project' in the Cape Town section and download the free geotagged soundtrack. Use a handsfree kit or play through your car sound system using Bluetooth or an auxiliary cable.

Once you're in your car, open The Endemic Project in the app and push START before you set off. In the 'Start route' menu, select 'YES' and listen to the instructions (this is a good time to set the volume). Leave the app running and drive past Kirstenbosch Gardens en route to Hout Bay. After the bottom gate main entrance, continue on to the T-junction and turn right. The soundtrack will start automatically as you go up the hill. The route distance is five kilometres and the tour takes about six minutes. For the best experience, drive the route at night at 50km/h.

ORANGE KLOOF

Table Mountain's best and most exclusive hiking

Constantia Nek, Hout Bay
SanParks area manager: 021-422-1601
Access only with a permit and a guide
Permits are free for groups of 6-12 max

The parking lot at the traffic circle at the top of Constantia Nek is the start of the easiest route up Table Mountain, reached by taking the road to the right as you face the mountain. To the left of the parking lot is another road, but this one is barred and bears a sign forbidding unauthorised access.

As the sign shows, Orange Kloof is a restricted part of Table Mountain National Park and a proclaimed wilderness area due to the indigenous Afro-montain forest growing there. Only 12 people a day are allowed in this lush and secluded valley; permit holders must be accompanied by an accredited guide or a member of the Mountain Club of South Africa (MCSA).

There are several hiking trails in the valley, but only one 'official' one. The Disa River Trail follows a level jeep track along the side of the valley before turning right, following the Disa River into a shady gorge, taking you past ferns, tempting swimming holes and moss-covered boulders to a lovely waterfall known as Hell's Gate.

Two other trails (Intake Ravine and Frustration Gorge) lead to the summit of the Twelve Apostles and Grootkop. Frustration Gorge was so named because, back in the 1930s, when members of the MCSA tried to create this route, they met an unclimbable section of sheer rock just 20 feet from the top. Thoroughly frustrated, they had to retreat in defeat. The route was eventually completed, but it is seldom hiked these days; if you decide to attempt it, you'll need an experienced guide.

Hiking in Orange Kloof offers one of the best and most exclusive Table Mountain hiking experiences: indigenous forest, pristine fynbos, glorious views and total solitude.

NEARBY
Myburgh's Waterfall Ravine

If the idea of organising a permit and a guide doesn't appeal to you, Myburgh's Waterfall Ravine, accessible from a trail starting at the end of Farrier's Way in Hout Bay, offers a similarly solitary hiking experience. The strenuous scramble up the back of the mountain, through a ravine that boasts a beautiful waterfall, is famous for being one of the best places to see the Table Mountain disa (*Disa uniflora*). This red orchid, which flowers between January and March, is rare and strictly protected; the cool, wet cliffs near the waterfall are their ideal habitat.

DE HEL

The jewel of Constantia's green spaces

Entrance on Southern Cross Drive, near intersection with Monterey Drive
Access between sunrise and sunset
Free entry

Winding through the opulent houses of Constantia is a network of nine public walking trails. Known as the Constantia Green Belt, these easy English countryside-style walks span meadows, streams and shady forests. Some are well known to local residents, but others are almost entirely unfrequented. The De Hel Nature Area is probably the least visited but also the largest and most historically interesting.

Situated on the slopes below Constantia Nek, this lush valley was first used as a buitepost (outpost) by the Dutch East India Company in 1714, when it was known as the Wittebomen post. The river running off the mountain provided a perennial water source for the orchards and gardens established here. Its fine trees made it one of four sites that the company relied upon to provide timber for building and ship repairs.

Ancient cattle tracks established by Khoikhoi pastoralists would have passed through this site and it is thought that there may be unmarked burial sites here. The valley was also used as a way station for runaway slaves. Thanks to its rich history, the 21-hectare area was declared a Provincial Heritage Site in 2012.

While most walkers stick to the level jeep track skirting the valley, it's worth descending into the glen to explore the overgrown jungle of trees, vines, ferns and giant impaties – a rare surviving remnant of the natural forest of the region. Two hidden paths lead down into it and a tangle of trails meander to 'The Meadow', a flat piece of land where woodcutters' cottages once stood. Some of the fruit trees and garden plants once cultivated remain. If it weren't for the sounds of traffic passing on the road above, you could easily believe yourself lost in a subtropical jungle.

An added attraction is the presence of some of the Cape's most elusive birds. The secretive Knysna warbler is a common resident in the thickets beside the streams; if you're lucky, you may spot it creeping around in the undergrowth or hear its beautiful trilling song. The buff-spotted flufftail is another legendary skulker whose call can be heard here in the evenings, along with those of the wood owl, spotted eagle owl and fiery-necked nightjar. Cape clawless otter and western leopard toad also live here.

Be aware that, as it is usually deserted, it is unwise to walk alone.

De Hel has nothing to do with hell, but is a corruption of De Hellen, Dutch for 'the slope' – a most accurate description.

THE PORTRAIT OF DR BARRY

A woman disguised as a man for 56 years in order to be a doctor

Alphen Boutique Hotel
Alphen Drive
Constantia

Several notable paintings hang in a conference room at the Alphen Hotel, including a large and spectacular canvas by Penny Siopis. But one picture is oddly amateurish; it depicts a rather sour-looking red-haired man in British Army uniform. Unimpressive as it appears, this is one of very few portraits of the enigmatic and extraordinary Dr James Barry.

Dr Barry arrived at the Cape in 1817 to take up a posting as staff surgeon to the British garrison. The unusually short 28-year-old MD had graduated from Edinburgh University five years earlier and joined the British Army. Aside from his height and high-pitched voice, Dr Barry was chiefly remarkable for his exceptional skill and terrible temper.

The former was demonstrated during his performance of one of the earliest successful Caesarian sections, in which both mother and child survived. The child was named James Barry Munnik and later became the godfather of James Barry Munnik Hertzog, the third Prime Minister of the Union of South Africa. Dr Barry also made improvements to Cape Town's water system, insisted on better medical care for lepers and prisoners, and pioneered sanitary conditions in hospitals.

Dr Barry's ability was matched only by his irascibility. On being asked to attend a clergyman with toothache, he sent a farrier instead, with instructions that "there was a donkey that needed a tooth pulled." He also famously duelled Josias Cloete at the Alphen (which is still owned by the Cloetes). Later, in the Crimea, he was so rude to Florence Nightingale that she called him "the most hardened creature I ever met."

But perhaps neither Dr Barry's contributions to medical care in the Cape, where he served until 1828, nor his many eccentricities would have been as well-remembered had it not transpired that he was, in fact, a she.

It was only after Dr Barry died of dysentery in London in 1865 that the charwoman attending his body visited Dr Barry's doctor claiming the deceased had been 'a perfect female'. However, Dr Barry had already been buried and the army, wishing to evade scandal, sealed his records for 100 years.

It was only very recently that a scholar found documentary evidence proving that Dr Barry had been born Margaret Anne Bulkley in 1789. She had disguised herself as a man in 1809 in order to study medicine – a profession forbidden to women in Britain until 1876. Dr Barry's deception, which she maintained for 56 years, made her the first qualified female physician in British history – and probably its most daring.

THE KRAMAT
AT KLEIN CONSTANTIA

The long lost shrine of a Muslim saint in exile

Klein Constantia Road, Constantia
Visitors of all faiths are welcome, but should cover their heads, remove their
shoes and sit or stand respectfully, facing the grave
24 hours a day, year round
Free entry

Just to the right of the gateway to Klein Constantia wine estate is a long, narrow driveway with a signpost to a kramat (shrine). Drive down it and you'll find a small parking lot and what looks like a miniature mosque sheltered by a grove of old oak trees beside a stream. This is the kramat of Sheikh Abdurahman Matebe Shah, a Muslim saint and an 'Orange Cayen' – a man of influence, considered dangerous by the Dutch East India Company.

When the Dutch conquered Sumatra, Matebe Shah was banished and sent to the Cape, along with his fellow Auliyah (friend of Allah), Sayed Mahmud. They became the first political exiles here. Unknown to the Dutch, however, Matebe Shah was also what is known as a *hafez* – a holy man who has memorised the Quran down to the last comma – and he immediately set about teaching the Cape's Muslim slaves.

The sheik arrived in the Cape Colony in 1667 and is thought to have died between 1681 and 1685. The story told by the shrine's caretaker goes that nobody knew where he had died, so his body was lost for more than 100 years. This was a tragedy for the Islamic community, as the remains of Muslim saints are believed to possess sacred powers.

One day, when the farm's owner ordered his workers to till the plot beside the stream, one section of earth kept mysteriously rising above the ground around it. It was eventually discovered to contain the remains of Matebe Shah. The farmer was told about the site's great significance and asked to grant the local Muslim community access to it. He refused, and a series of unfortunate events dogged him until he was forced to give up the farm entirely. The new owner proved more amenable and the imam was honoured at last.

Initially, only a humble wooden shack marked the site, but this was later replaced by the current building, with its distinctive green domed roof. It was designed by Gawie Fagan, one of Cape Town's leading architects, and constructed by the Cape Mazaar Society.

A Prophecy Dating Back About 250 Years

The area around a kramat is thought to be especially peaceful. Legend has it that they are protected from fire, flood and other disasters. There's also a prophecy dating back about 250 years that the Cape's Muslims would be protected by a 'circle of kramats'. According to local beliefs, the circle is now complete.

DIE OOG

26

A microcosm of Cape wildlife and breeding site for an endangered toad

Corner of Lakewood and Midwood Avenues, Bergvliet
Daily 7am–7pm
Free entry

A small, apparently unremarkable dam and a hidden wetland deep in the sleepy suburb of Bergvliet are among the few remaining breeding grounds of the endangered western leopard toad (*Amietophrynus pantherinus*). The ancient dam is actually built around a spring (hence the name 'Die Oog' – 'The Eye/Spring' in Afrikaans) and dates back almost 300 years to when Bergvliet Farm was established here in 1726.

Dr Frederick Purcell, curator of the South African Museum, lived on Bergvliet Farm in 1904 and collected more than 600 species of indigenous plants here. Later owners, the Eksteens, converted the dam into a recreational lake, introducing swans and even creating an artificial island built of ironstone in its centre. Fortunately, when the farm was subdivided for a housing development in 1982, the dam and a surrounding area, just 1.2 hectares (3 acres) in size, was designated as a bird sanctuary by the city.

Tiny as the reserve is, it has four quite different ecosystems. A small but unique area of granite fynbos on the eastern boundary has been cordoned off. In summer this area blooms with rare geophytes, and in autumn with Erica verticillata, which is classified as 'extinct in the wild' but has been reintroduced here.

The dam is a major urban feeding and roosting site for waterfowl. On winter evenings the island can hold as many as 1,000 birds, including coots, moorhens, cattle egrets and sacred ibises. Other birds resident at Die Oog include spotted thick-knee (dikkop), weaver, guinea fowl, Karoo prinia and pintailed whydah.

The surrounding grassland contains trees, shrubs and reeds that provide habitat and shelter for a variety of other fauna, including porcupine, Cape clawless otter, water mongoose, angulate tortoise and dwarf chameleon. During spring and summer, indigenous marsh terrapins can be seen sunning themselves on the rocks around the island.

However, it is during the cold, wet month of August that Die Oog truly comes to life, as the seasonal wetland reverberates with the roars and snores of the western leopard toads, which return by their hundreds to breed at this site every year. The toads, braving busy roads, usually arrive between late July and early August; their mating calls can be heard throughout the month. By mid September, the dam is full of tadpoles, which, about a month later, have grown into tiny toadlets the size of a fingernail. The young toads will leave Die Oog towards the end of the year, with luck to return again the next.

POLLSMOOR MESS

27

A public restaurant in a maximum security prison

Pollsmoor Maximum Security Prison
Steenberg Road
Tokai
Monday–Saturday 7.30am–2pm
No alcohol served
Credit cards not accepted

Even the most knowledgeable foodies in Cape Town are unlikely to have dined at this particular eatery, but that's not because the food is lousy. On the contrary, it's delicious: fresh and prepared to perfection. The portions are sizeable and the service is friendly. Moreover, it's astonishingly cheap – lunch for two comes to less than R100 – and tipping isn't allowed.

But, although Pollsmoor Mess (recently renamed Idlanathi) has been open to the public for well over a decade, few Capetonians ever eat here or even know of its existence. Perhaps that's because it's not particularly well advertised, hidden as it is behind the high walls, razor wire and guard posts of one of Cape Town's most notorious jails.

Pollsmoor Maximum Security Prison is incongruously situated in the wealthy, leafy suburb of Tokai, and is large enough to qualify as a suburb in itself. Famous inmates have included Nelson Mandela, Walter Sisulu and Alan Boesak. The prison houses some of South Africa's most dangerous criminals, including many members of the infamous Numbers Gangs.

Idlanathi means 'eat with us' (in Zulu). Although the fact that all the cooks and waiters are inmates might give you pause, these are low-security prisoners due for release; Idlanathi is part of a rehabilitation and skills-training programme. Despite the undeniably institutional atmosphere, the warm welcome you receive from your waiter will soon put you at ease.

The restaurant is open for breakfast and lunch, with a menu offering the usual pub fare, such as fish and chips, curries and burgers, as well as some traditional African meals. The chicken schnitzel (R37) is highly recommended. If you don't feel like sitting down, you can order takeaways.

To find it, simply go to the main gate and tell the guards you are going to the restaurant. They will direct you to the Pollsmoor Recreation Centre, where you can park right outside. There's no need to book in advance.

Also, be careful about where you point your camera. Taking photos of your food, yourself and the inside of the restaurant is okay, but for security and privacy reasons be sure not to photograph any prisoners or guards.

South Peninsula

MILKWOOD FOREST

Ancient wood on the slopes of Chapman's Peak

Noordhoek
021-789-8000
Much of the forest lies within the grounds of Monkey Valley Resort
Open to the public

At the north end of Long Beach, on the lower slopes of Chapman's Peak, lies a small milkwood (*Sideroxylon inerme*) forest. Relatively sheltered from the prevailing southeaster, the trees have grown to substantial sizes. These slow-growing coastal trees have dense foliage, black berries and small white flowers.

Since developers have decimated milkwood forests throughout the Cape, this is a treasured wood. The rootstock of the Noordhoek trees is thought to be up to 2,000 years old and some of the current stands date back some 400 years.

The most beautiful part of the forest lies within Monkey Valley Resort, formerly a farm. Jan Hesterman, the first owner of the land, gave the place its name. He was newly arrived from Holland and not familiar with African animals. When he saw baboons gamboling up the ravine, he named his land Monkey Valley.

When the farm was transformed into a resort, guest cottages were designed to occupy spaces between the trees. To blend into the forest, only natural materials were used and most of the log-and-thatched cottages are on stilts. Some even have milkwood trunks growing through their decks.

Due to their high moisture content, milkwoods don't easily ignite, so they act as a natural firebreak and are resistant to the Cape's notorious veld fires. Indeed, a number of devastating blazes have swept through Chapman's Peak and Noordhoek in recent years, but this forest has remained intact, despite having burning foliage rain down on it from the mountain above.

Milkwoods are 'sociable' trees and don't like to grow on their own. It is said that a lone tree often does not last long after its 'companions' have been removed. This is possibly due to the fact that milkwoods grow from underground rootstock, which can be damaged when companion trees are cut down.

Before developers got hold of Noordhoek, the forest stretched down to the beach parking lot and you could park your car in the shade of milkwoods. However, in the 1980s, a property development company from Johannesburg bought the land and sent in bulldozers to clear the site. For three months, dismayed Noordhoek residents saw their forest vanishing before their eyes. Fortunately, the development was stopped and the remainder of the forest saved.

WRECK OF THE SS *KAKAPO*

Legend has it that Captain Nicolayson continued to live on the wreck for three years

Long Beach, Kommetjie
Walk south along Noordhoek Beach from Noordhoek car park
(1¼ hours) or north from the Wireless Road beach car park in Kommetjie
(30 minutes). The remains of the wreck lie high up on the beach.

Named after an endangered New Zealand parrot, the SS *Kakapo* was a 1,093-ton, schooner-rigged steamship, built in Grangemouth, Scotland in 1898. She was bought by the Union Steam Ship Company of New Zealand in 1900 and dispatched from Great Britain via the Cape under the command of a Danish captain, Niels Nicolayson.

On 25 May 1900 the SS *Kakapo* put into Cape Town Harbour for coal and set sail the same afternoon, bound for Australia. The captain pressed on at her top speed of nine knots, despite an increasing northwesterly gale.

Driving rain, thick spray and huge swells drastically reduced the visibility. The officer-of-the-watch mistook Chapman's Peak for Cape Point and ordered a turn to the east. At 6.20pm the SS *Kakapo* ran aground just north of the mouth of the Wildevogelvlei. Strong wind and large waves drove the vessel far up the beach, where she settled in the soft sand.

Two crew members used a rope ladder to get to the beach and walked inland until they reached Brakkloof farm. The alarm was raised and the rest of the crew were rescued. Over the next week a number of attempts were made by a Cape Town tug to pull her off the beach, to no avail.

Captain Nicolayson chose to remain on board and refused to meet sightseers and reporters. His only communication was by means of messages stuck in bottles, which he hauled aboard by rope. He also refused to answer questions about the cause of the accident or to allow anyone on board.

Legend has it that he continued to live on the SS *Kakapo* for three years. A photograph from the period shows smoke coming from the funnel, the sand dunes building up around the wreck indicating that it had already been aground for some time. Other sources suggest that a vagrant had made a home in the wreck.

The boiler, rudder and ribs still protrude from the sand and make for a haunting sight. The wreck was featured in *Ryan's Daughter*, an Academy Award winning film directed by David Lean.

SLANGKOP LIGHTHOUSE

Cape Town's highest lantern

Lighthouse Road, Kommetjie
021-783-1717
Daily 10am–3pm

Slangkop is the tallest lighthouse on the South African coastline. It's a graceful structure set above the rocks on the Kommetjie shore and comprises a 33-metre circular tower with various administrative and diesel-generator buildings around its base. The lantern houses a revolving electric light that flashes four times every 30 seconds and has a range of 33 nautical miles.

In the building beside the tower there's a small museum to lighthouses that's worth a visit. Then ascend the tower's spiral staircase until you reach the beautiful lantern. If it's not too windy, step out onto the balcony for breath-taking views of Kommetjie.

The tower was erected as a result of the findings of the Lighthouse Commission, appointed by Sir Francis Hely-Hutchinson in 1906. Sir Francis, governor of the Cape, called for proposals to improve safety measures for shipping around the Cape coast.

The commission's recommendations included the urgent construc-

ion of a lighthouse at Slangkop due to the many wrecks that occurred between Table Bay and Cape Point. Ships leaving Cape Town soon lost sight of the Robben Island Light and had to pass Duiker Point before coming into range of the Cape Point Light. Furthermore, Cape Point was often shrouded by cloud or mist. The erection of a lighthouse at Kommetjie was the ideal solution. It was also recommended that the light be positioned close to the waterline, rather than up on the hill, where it would be frequently blanketed by fog.

In 1913 tenders were invited by WT Douglas, consulting engineer to the high commissioner of the Union. The tower was constructed from cast-iron segments weighing 500kg each. When completed, it stood 30 metres tall from the ground to the gallery. The original specification stipulated that the date '1914' be cast above the doorway. No one could have foreseen that World War I would interfere with the plan.

The lighthouse was eventually commissioned on 4 March 1919. In 1936, a 4kW electric lamp was installed, increasing the candlepower to 16,750,000cd. The lighting equipment has since been replaced and has slightly reduced power.

Being close to civilisation on a beautiful stretch of coast, Slangkop has been a popular station for lighthouse-keeping families. Although now fully automated, the facility is still manned for security reasons and to allow visitors.

IMHOFF'S GIFT HOMESTEAD

The gift of a farm to an industrious lady

Driving south towards Kommetjie on Kommetjie Road (M65), Imhoff Farm is at the traffic-light intersection (Milky Way) opposite the entrance to Ocean View
021-783-4545

Beside the main road leading into Kommetjie, Imhoff Farm comprises a cluster of Cape Dutch buildings. The old homestead boasts sash windows, a vine pergola and a restaurant. The property also has a farmyard geared for children. The stables, silo, smithy and slave quarters are occupied by artists as well as furniture, craft and food shops.

Imhoff Farm has an intriguing history. During the early years of the Cape colony, ships anchored in Table Bay were battered by northwesterly gales during the winter months. Heavy losses were incurred as vessels were driven ashore or sunk. In 1741, the directors of the Dutch East India Company decided that Simon's Bay would provide a much safer winter anchorage. However, this bay is a long way from Cape Town and it was going to be difficult supplying fresh victuals to a fleet based there.

Nevertheless, in 1743 Baron Gustav Wilhelm van Imhoff, Commissioner Extraordinaire at the Cape, ordered the construction of the Simon's Bay refreshment station. Land in the Fish Hoek and Noordhoek valleys was made available to cultivate and supply fresh produce.

Frederick Rosseau, owner of the farm *Zwaansweide*, was a wealthy member of the Burgher Council and one of the landowners who provisioned the wintering ships. He developed and improved the farm. His wife Christina continued the good work after he died. Baron van Imhoff was so impressed with Christina Rosseau's output that he awarded her a gift of land near Slangkop. The area became known as Imhoff's Gift.

Pierre Rocher took over the farm in 1815, extending its boundaries to include the salt pans at Chapman's Bay. Later in the 19th century, the farm was subdivided and a piece of land now known as Ocean View was sold to Albert de Villiers. (This property, as well as a portion of Imhoff's Gift, was expropriated in 1966 for the creation of a suburb for coloured people.) In 1912, prominent Cape businessman Johannes van der Horst acquired the farm and it has remained in his family ever since.

Imhoff's Gift was ravaged by a bushfire in 1958. The homestead was badly damaged and two wooden figureheads – salvaged from shipwrecks and given pride of place at the entrance – were destroyed.

PEERS CAVE

5

The cave the world forgot

Silvermine Nature Reserve
Table Mountain National Park
*To reach the cave, take Ou Kaapse Weg towards Fish Hoek. Pass the turn-off
to Noordhoek and park in the car park on the left, where the road bends right.
Follow the path up the small koppie and then right, hugging the cliff. The walk
takes about 30 minutes*
Free entry

In 1927 two amateur naturalists, the Australian immigrant Victor Peers and his son Bertie, came across stone tools in a rock shelter above the Fish Hoek sand dunes. Encouraged by John Goodwin, an archaeologist at the University of Cape Town who had abandoned the site in 1925 because of its 'inconvenience', the Peers began to dig.

Excavating Skildergat (as the cave was then known) was difficult; the pair used spades, picks and even dynamite. Near the surface was a deep shell midden, indicating higher historical sea levels. Lower down were the remains of eight human skeletons, along with an iron spearhead indicating they'd been buried within the era of European contact with the Cape. However, it was a ninth skeleton, identified as a man of around 30, who became a local celebrity. 'Fish Hoek Man' had the largest brain of any human so far discovered and was estimated to be 15,000 years old – researches in the 1990s revealed that he had actually lived in the Later Stone Age, around 12,000 B.P.

These finds created so much interest that a 1929 newspaper report said visiting British and South African scientists "went direct from the mail steamer to the cave before going anywhere else." Field Marshal Smuts declared that "it promises to be the most remarkable cave site yet found in South Africa."

But the site's scientific value had been diminished by the Peers' relatively primitive excavation methods and their poor record keeping. Furthermore, no effort was made to protect it and many visitors carried off artifacts or graffitied its walls. The tragedy is that it was discovered too early, before archeology was properly established in South Africa. Archaeologists have called it "the cave the world forgot."

Miraculously, the cave's rock paintings – the only ones within a 100-kilometre radius of the Cape Peninsula – survived. The yellow and brown patterns of dots, lines and handprints are still visible above the graffiti.

NEARBY

The Fish Hoek Museum

Tuesday–Saturday 9.30am–12.30pm

One of the three rooms in this little museum is dedicated to Peers Cave, with photographs of the excavation and some stone tools. (Fish Hoek Man himself is in the South African Museum.)

HET POSTHUYS MUSEUM

6

The oldest extant settler building in South Africa

Between Muizenberg Station and the SAPS Museum
Main Road
Muizenberg
021-788-7972

Between Muizenberg Station and the SAPS Museum, on the Main Road of Muizenberg, 'Het Posthuys' is a simple building erected in 1673 by the Dutch East India Company. Used as a signal station and military observation post to warn the colony of attack from the sea, it is believed to be the oldest extant settler building in South Africa. It is certainly the oldest in False Bay.

The Anglo-American Corporation, together with historians, archaeologists and City architect Dirk Visser, began its restoration in 1979. Archaeological work uncovered a two-stuiwer coin (minted in Holland in 1680) and a flintlock musket, along with a horde of other artefacts.

The restoration involved returning the Posthuys to its 17th-century appearance as a single-storey dwelling. All later additions were removed, a thatch roof and brandsolder (fireproof ceiling) were reinstated, shell-lime floors laid, stone steps rebuilt, and new doors, casement windows and shutters installed.

Due to hostilities between Holland and England in the late 17th century, this site was chosen for the erection of a watch post to guard False Bay. The building was part of a larger barracks complex. There is some debate whether the current edifice is, in fact, the original structure.

The buildings on this site remained in military use throughout the 18th century. During the Battle of Muizenberg in 1795, the Posthuys received a direct cannon-ball hit on its stoep. Adjoining buildings appear to have been destroyed at the time. The site was still in military use during the first British occupation and during Batavian rule.

By 1814, the troops stationed here had been removed and the Posthuys was occupied by a sergeant in charge of convicts, who were housed in the adjoining barracks and employed in road making.

During the 1840s the structure was rented out as holiday accommodation. By the 1880s, JA Stegmann of Claremont obtained a lease for the property and upgraded it for use as a holiday home, calling it *Stegmann's Rust*.

By 1919 the barracks had fallen into ruin and were demolished, leaving the Posthuys as sole survivor of the early military post. It was upgraded in 1922 for accommodation by the Union Defence Force. Seven years later the building was sold to W Leon, who made various additions and in turn sold it to Anglo-American in 1969.

The Posthuys was accorded national monument status in 1980 and has since been used as a museum by the Muizenberg Historical Conservation Society.

THE CUPID AT CASA LABIA

A mistake made by one of Europe's most important 18th-century painters

192 Main Road, Muizenberg
Tuesday–Sunday 10am–4pm; closed on Mondays
Free entry

On either side of the ballroom doors in Casa Labia hang two tapestry designs by France's most famous artist of the Rococo period, François Boucher. The one on the right reveals a secret: Madame de Pompadour's favourite painter made a bit of a booboo.

The painting, entitled 'Love's Offering', depicts Cupid pointing at a statue of himself. But what neither Cupid nor Boucher himself seem to have realised is that the statue of Cupid has two left feet. No one knows why the mistake was made, but Casa Labia's curator likes to speculate that the painter was distracted by the beauty of the ladies in Madame de Pompadour's salon.

Nonetheless, the Labias must have enjoyed the flawed painting as there is a hand-coloured engraving of it in the next room. Due to the smaller size of the copy, it's not possible to see whether the engraver corrected the error in the original.

While its name (like the Labia Cinema in the City Centre) may sometimes give rise to giggles, Casa Labia, set between the seaside and the mountain on the main road between Muizenberg and Kalk Bay, is a beautiful building with a noble history.

Count Natale Labia was a Venetian nobleman sent to South Africa in 1916 as the Italian consul. He married Ida, the daughter of the Randlord JB Robinson, and was later appointed Italy's first minister plenipotentiary.

In 1930, the Labias built Casa Labia to be both the embassy and a family home. They wanted to give it a Venetian flavour – creating a southern reflection of the Palazzo Labia, which stands on the Cannaregio Canal in Venice. The furniture, chandeliers, mirrors, ceiling panels and wall fabrics were all imported from Venice, along with an interior decorator. The count even shipped over a gondola and gondolier, but the Cape weather immediately rendered this idea impractical.

The house was decorated with various pieces selected from the Labia family's priceless art collection, including works by François Boucher. As a key artist of the Rococo Period, Boucher's sentimental, pink and blue toned paintings of pastoral and mythical scenes helped to define the style of that century. He also designed many tapestries for the Beauvais Tapestry works, for which these two designs were intended.

The Casa Labia art collection also features several English and Italian masters as well as contemporary works by South African artists such as Irma Stern, Gerard Sekoto and John Muafangejo. Upstairs is an art gallery featuring exhibitions by contemporary local artists.

MUIZENBERG STATION

The city's only teak clock tower

Just above Muizenberg Beach on Main Road

With its elegant teak clock tower, Muizenberg Station is the prettiest railway station on the Cape Town to Simon's Town line. This grand building is the symbolic gateway to False Bay, marking the start of arguably the most scenic railway line in South Africa. Designed by a pupil of Sir Herbert Baker, the fine proportions and generosity of its interior spaces are a typical example of glamorous Edwardian architecture.

Today, this red brick structure with arched sandstone entrances graces the skyline of Muizenberg as it did a century ago. The stairs and paving are of quarry flagstone from Elsie's Peak, Fish Hoek, while the dressed sandstone is from Kalk Bay. The interiors, with their original high ceilings and wooden floors, transport you back to an era when men in black suits and top hats enjoyed tea on the station's open-air balcony. Make sure you don't miss the two cannons mounted on the seaside platform: a British 9-pounder (circa 1760) and a Swedish 24-pounder (circa 1782).

With the growth of Muizenberg in the 19th century came the need for a station. The architectural department of South African Railways set about creating a statement in stone to acknowledge Muizenberg's importance as the Cape's first 'beach resort' town – the Brighton of South Africa. With the arrival of the railway in 1883, thousands of day-trippers now had access to the seaside – previously the sole privilege of the wealthy, who owned horses and traps.

The building we see today is not the original station, but rather one that replaced the simple structure of the 1880s. The new station was opened by the Minister of Transport, the Honourable Henry Burton, on 7 June 1913. The original plans show a booking office, station-master and station foreman's offices, a porter's office, luggage rooms, cloakrooms, rest room and toilets.

A few years later, the decorative wrought iron balustrade on the balconies was replaced with brickwork due to the corrosive effects of the sea and strong southeasterly winds. All embellishments and ironwork were removed to make the building maintenance-free. The upstairs rooms were also converted into a residence for the stationmaster and his family.

This grand old lady of the suburban line was declared a national monument in 1981. However, the building continued to deteriorate. In 1991 all commuter stations, including Muizenberg, fell under the control of the newly formed SARCC (SA Rail Commuter Corporation). Extensive renovations were conducted in 1992.

BATTLE OF MUIZENBERG COMMEMORATION BOARD AND FLAGPOLES

First British invasion of the Cape

Small parking lot opposite Bailey's Cottage
Main Road, Muizenberg

On 7 August 1795 British warships sailed towards Muizenberg to challenge the Dutch defenders there. The home force had only two cannons mounted in a fortification on the hillside above Muizenberg.

Casa Labia, the ornate Venetian-style palazzo that today houses a restaurant, stands beside the remains of the earthen fortification, now overgrown with grass. This was the site of the Dutch gun emplacement. About 100 metres to the south of the palazzo, on the mountain opposite

Bailey's Cottage, are the remains of trenches used in the skirmish. Look out for the signboard and two flagpoles (at the back of a small parking lot opposite Bailey's Cottage) that commemorate the battle.

During the attack, four British warships fired 800 cannonballs in the space of half an hour. Some of these are still buried in the mountainside. In addition, British soldiers and sailors who'd landed in Simon's Town marched on the fortification from the south along what is today Main Road.

The Dutch didn't expect an attack from warships, so their two 24-pound cannons were trained on the road. None of the Dutch defenders was injured by the British cannon fire and they hastily turned their 24-pounders on the ships. A lucky shot struck a British cannon on board HMS *America*, killing five crewmen. However, the Dutch position was tenuous and, after a brief defence, they spiked their cannons and retreated to positions inland.

The two sides continued skirmishing for the next month. On 14 September, British reinforcements arrived and about 5,000 men left Muizenberg for Cape Town. The Dutch surrendered, heralding the beginning of the first British occupation.

A failure in communication

The background to this battle lies in the situation in Europe. The Cape was in the hands of the Dutch, operating as a refreshment station for the merchant fleet of the Dutch East India Company. As far as the local commander knew, Holland and Britain were still allies in a war against France, so there was no reason not to welcome British warships at the Cape. But unknown to Cape Commissioner-General, Abraham Sluysken, Holland had been overrun by Napoleon, which meant all Dutch colonies now belonged to France. Had Napoleon taken possession of the Cape, it would have threatened Britain's access to the East. Exploiting the lack of communications, British Admiral George Elphinstone neglected to mention that Holland and Britain were now on opposing sides, so the Dutch continued tolerating them until they attacked.

RHODES COTTAGE MUSEUM

Deathbed of an empire builder

246 Main Road, Muizenberg
021-788-1816 (phone to check if open)
Free entry, donations welcome

The room immediately to your left as you enter Rhodes Cottage Museum is where Cecil John Rhodes (1853-1902) died. It's a humble space with a small iron bedstead – hardly the deathbed you'd expect of one of the world's richest and most powerful men. On the wall is an old map of Rhodesia, the country named after him. Above the fireplace hangs a brooding portrait of the man himself.

During the last days of his life, the weather was extremely hot and a hole was broken into the wall (where the map now hangs) to allow Rhodes to breathe more easily. The rest of the house has exhibits depicting his life, including photographs, newspaper cuttings and caricatures revealing the man behind the legacy.

Rhodes was a controversial British imperialist, businessman, mining magnate, politician and one-time prime minister of the Cape Colony. He was also co-founder of De Beers diamond-mining company. Rhodes was an ardent believer in British imperialism and used his influence to colonise the lands north of the Limpopo River, which were renamed Rhodesia.

In 1899, he purchased this simple, three-bedroomed cottage in Muizenberg with its lovely garden and smaller cottage used by caretakers and staff. His health was not good and he wanted the rejuvenating influence of sea breezes. Rhodes preferred this cottage to his other residences, including his Groote Schuur mansion in Rondebosch. He was a man of simple tastes and the furniture was austere: look for the long conference table, which comes from the boardroom at De Beers, and the wooden chest in which he carried all his worldly belongings from England to South Africa.

Rhodes spent his last days in the cottage before succumbing to heart failure at the young age of 48. His corpse was transported to a burial place he'd chosen in the Matopos Hills of Zimbabwe. There's a diorama of this site in one of the back rooms of the cottage.

After his death, the cottage remained in the possession of Rhodes's trustees until it was donated to the Northern Rhodesian Government in 1932. It passed into the hands of the City of Cape Town in 1937 on condition that it be kept as a memorial to Rhodes. The following year it was declared a national monument.

ST JAMES MILESTONE

A beautiful witness from the history of road development and transportation in the 19th century

Located opposite 30 Main Road, close to the corner of Braemar Road, St James (Milestone XVI on Google Maps)

On the ocean side of the old wagon road (today called Main Road) from Cape Town towards Simon's Town, a dark grey stone stands on the pavement facing the sea – clearly marked in Roman Numerals "XVI miles from The Town House", (so 16 miles from the Town House, Greenmarket Square), this is the so-called Saint James Milestone.

Dating from the 19th century, this milestone is one of twenty four milestones that were installed along the main road from Cape Town to Simon's Town during 1814-1815 under the governorship of Lord Charles Somerset. Milestones had already been used in England for several decades.

These milestones served to mark the edge of the road and provided accurate distance markers so that travel times and fares could be calculated for both the transport of people and postal services. People would use them as meeting points and as addresses, when referring to a property being located close to a milestone. They were made of Malmsbury slate sourced from Robben Island.

Initially, this road was a sand track established during the middle of the 18th century when ships were docking in the more sheltered bay of Simon's Town during winter, and produce needed to be transported to and from Cape Town. Travel was limited to horseback or wagon, taking most of the day. Funds were never available to upgrade the road until the second British occupation era, when in 1807 Louis Thibault was commissioned to inspect and make recommendations for repairs. To generate funding, the government sold plots alongside the road, and city dwellers started to take advantage of the idea of living along this coastal route.

The investment in upgrading this road certainly reaped rewards and became significantly important after 1814 when the navy was transferred permanently to Simon's Town.

Today the drive from Cape Town to Simon's Town takes around an hour: prior to this, the same journey could have taken up to two days.

The other remaining milestones

As the name implies, these milestones were placed on the side of the road every mile from the Town House in Greenmarket Square for twenty-four miles. Although some have gone missing, there are still several still in situ: Rondebosch (V miles), Kenilworth (VII miles), Wynberg (VIII miles), Plumstead (IX miles) Tokai (XII miles), Kirstenhof (XIII miles), Lakeside (XV miles), Kalk Bay – replica (XVII miles) and Fishhoek (XIX miles).

HOLY TRINITY CHURCH

The most beautiful church on False Bay

42 Main Road
Kalk Bay
021-788-1641

With its steep thatched roof and sandstone walls, Holy Trinity Church is a picturesque place of worship that sits in a seaside churchyard. It's a peaceful sanctuary beside Kalk Bay's busy Main Road. At the time of its consecration, *The Church News* described it as "the most perfect church in the diocese."

Holy Trinity (constructed in 1873-74) is a fine example of mid-Victorian church architecture and very little has been altered in the intervening century and a half. It was built by John Gainsford of Newlands and financed by three renowned benefactors of Kalk Bay: sisters Harriet and Charlotte Humphreys and Alice Pocklington. They raised £1,500 to cover the cost of the building and its fine interior fittings.

The architect was Henry Woodyer, a London gentleman who'd designed many churches in England, some of which the Humphreys sisters had visited. The ochre sandstone used in the construction of Holy Trinity came from quarries in St James and Fish Hoek and was donated by Thomas Cutting, a local hotelier and omnibus owner. The lych-gate at the churchyard entrance (1875) was the first of its kind in South Africa.

Charlotte Humphreys also bought Bishop Gray's holiday home on the south side of the property and donated the building for use as a rectory. In 1919 a memorial plaque was unveiled near the entrance to the church in memory of the three benefactors, who had returned to England in 1877.

The interior houses a large baptismal font made of marble, donated by businessman George John Nicholls in memory of his two daughters, Emma and Madeline, who drowned off Danger Beach in 1874. The font's sides are carved with the symbols of the Passion of Jesus and the emblems of the four Evangelists.

The nave's lovely windows are of quarry glass and were the work of James Powell and Sons of Whitefriars, London. The choir screen is made of teak and forms a second memorial to the drowned sisters. The encaustic tiles in the sanctuary were made by the firm Herbert Minton at Stoke-on-Trent in the English Potteries District. The reredos, which consists of marble and majolica tiles and mosaic work, is also from Mintons.

The wonderful sense of harmony throughout the interior can be attributed to the fact that most of the contemporary fittings were designed by Woodyer himself.

DALEBROOK TIDAL POOL

A beautiful little-known tidal pool

Opposite Dalebrook Café, 20 Main Road, Kalk Bay

Coming from Muizenberg, as you pass St James and head towards Kalk Bay, you will notice a bench high up on the ocean side that makes a great viewing point. Adjacent to this bench is a narrow stairway with steps down to a short tunnel going under the railway line. A few steps later and you will find yourself at Dalebrook Tidal Pool, the first to be built along the Muizenberg to Kalk Bay coastline.

Not easily visible while driving, the Dalebrook Tidal Pool is therefore much less known than the tidal pool at St James (with the beach huts). This stand-alone tidal pool, surrounded by rocks with beautiful views of Simon's Town in the distance, also has a certain quaint charm and is relatively uncrowded.

In 1903, the construction of the Dalebrook Tidal Pool was a sort of private enterprise without permission from the Kalk Bay-Muizenberg municipality. There are conflicting stories as to whether it was funded alone by local resident Mr Steer of Douglas Cottage, or whether additional residents also contributed. Either way, they started with the construction of a sea wall on the Muizenberg side. However, by the time it came to the other side, the money had run out (Steer blamed the municipality for his increased costs as he was forced to build to their requirements) and the tidal pool remained unfinished.

Three years later and many frustrated residents complaining about a half-finished pool, the municipality agreed to clean and complete the west wall. Finally in 1907, the Dalebrook tidal pool was open for bathing. It remained a small bathing pool until the 1960s, when the pool was expanded to the size you see today.

For years, the City of Cape Town has been cleaning the tidal pools by draining them, scraping seaweed and algae off the walls and treating them using a mix of chemicals. However, as tidal pools are also a sanctuary for fish, octopuses and striking purple nudibranchs, in 2017 a group of marine-loving citizens were determined to find a new chemical-free solution for cleaning these pools that would benefit both local swimmers and marine-life.

With crowd-funding efforts, the Dalebrook tidal pool was the first to experience the new cleaning method of high-pressure blasting, clearing algae from the walls using salt water – no more use of fresh water or chemicals.

Today pool cleaning is conducted every 28 days to coincide with spring tide: this means that the tops of the walls are much less slippery.

Due to the success of this project, all tidal pools within the City of Cape Town are now cleaned with this eco-friendly method.

THE FIRING OF THE 9-INCH GUN OF SIMON'S TOWN

19th-century naval artillery piece

Middle North Battery
One kilometre north of Simon's Town station (take the small, unmarked road
up the hill off Main Road opposite Lower North Battery)

The 9-inch gun north of Simon's Town station was designed in the mid-19th century as a broadside gun for ironclad warships and for the defence of harbours and sea fronts. It was built in 1865 and was the 22nd of 190 manufactured. The curious-looking weapon is muzzle-loaded and the barrel is rifled with six grooves. Its 9-inch shells had six corresponding rectangular protrusions made of lead that engaged with the barrel grooves to impart spin, stabilising the shell during flight.

The gun has a cast-steel barrel with a wrought-iron forged breech, cascable and trunnion, supported on a steel gun carriage, slide and mounting. It weighs 12.5 tons and could fire a 256-pound projectile up to a range of 6,000 yards at 1,440 feet per second.

This particular gun was first deployed in Halifax, Nova Scotia (until 1878), then on Bermuda (until 1881) and subsequently at Sheerness in England (until 1885). It was relocated to the Cape and mounted at Middle North Battery in 1896. The fortifications here had been established four years earlier to defend the nearby naval base. The gun was last fired operationally (three rounds) on 27 April 1903. It was decommissioned on 19 September 1906.

The gun, carriage, slide and mounting were restored in Simon's Town's East Dockyard Gun Shop in 1984. Despite missing some parts due to stripping by metal thieves, it's still in excellent condition. Warrant Officer Harry Croome, a member of the Cannon Association of South Africa (CAOSA), is the current custodian of the gun and spends much of his free time maintaining it.

The gun was fired again for the first time in 108 years on 16 March 2011. The South African Navy, in conjunction with CAOSA, have subsequently arranged for it to be fired on certain holidays. The public generally has about ten opportunities each year to witness this: three times during the SA Navy Festival in March, 27 April (Freedom Day), 16 June (Youth Day), 24 September (Heritage Day), 11 November (Remembrance Day), 16 December (Day of Reconciliation) and 31 December (New Year's Eve).

The 9-inch Guns of Scala Battery

Higher up the hill, above Middle North, you can spot the three, much larger 9-inch guns of Scala Battery, painted in camouflage patterns of different periods. These are of a later vintage, and served during both World Wars.

ROMAN ROCK LIGHTHOUSE

The only lighthouse in South Africa built on a site that is awash at high tide

About one kilometre off Simon's Town's naval-harbour wall

This lighthouse occupies a commanding position on an isolated outcrop in False Bay. Roman Rock was for centuries a treacherous hazard to ships entering Simon's Bay. This is the only lighthouse in South Africa to be built on a site that is awash at high tide.

The structure was designed by Alexander Gordon of the British Lighthouse Authority to replace a lightship that was anchored adjacent to the rock in the mid-19th century. Cast-iron segments were bolted together and the lowest ring secured to the rock. The stone was quarried at Seaforth Beach (from the boulders behind and beneath the present-day restaurant) and then ferried to Roman Rock.

In 1857 the ship Royal Saxon arrived in Simon's Town with the light's mechanism. Strong winds and high seas allowed for only 96 working days during the four-year period it took to complete the tower.

The light's first mechanism had a focal plane of 16.5 metres above high water and a range of 12 sea miles. Two keepers manned the lighthouse at all times and were relieved every seven days. A standby crew remained on shore as backup. The tower is narrow and cramped. Besides accommodation it also had to provide storage space for oil, water and supplies.

Keepers were confined to the tower for days at a time when the sea was rough. It was a boring job and they earned the highest salary in the lighthouse service. The only recreation was fishing, but reeling in a catch against the force of a strong southeaster required considerable skill.

In 1914 the light's mechanism was modernised and the tower no longer needed to be manned. Power was now supplied by dissolved acetylene gas stored in cylinders that were renewed every few months.

In 1992 the South African Navy requested that Roman Rock be electrified. By that stage, the bright urban lights encircling the shores of False Bay overpowered the lighthouse. An undersea cable was laid from the shore and the lighthouse was provided with a supplementary diesel engine and solar panels. The old lantern dome was removed to allow for a new optic and a glass-fibre replacement dome, which was airlifted to the lighthouse by a Sikorsky 861 helicopter.

AERIAL ROPEWAY

South Africa's first passenger ropeway

Simon's Town
*The most convenient viewing point is on St George's Street at the entrance to the
South African Naval Museum*

The row of grey, pyramid-shaped structures that can still be seen leading from the centre of Simon's Town to the top of Red Hill is all that remains of the old aerial ropeway. It was built at the beginning of the 20th century to service the Royal Navy's new hospital and sanatorium on Red Hill. The officer in charge of the naval dockyard suggested that the best way to convey patients from the town to the summit was via a ropeway.

The motivation reads: "The advantages of such a scheme are obvious: no obstruction to the traffic of any kind, less likelihood of the public catching any infectious diseases during the patient's transit to hospital and no wear and tear on the road leading to the hospital."

Plans for South Africa's first passenger ropeway were completed in 1902 (the only other ropeway at the time was used to transport material for the building of Simon's Town's dry dock). The works department began erecting standards made of tarred wood for carrying the wire rope, while vegetation was cleared to a width of 13 metres on either side of the route up the hillside.

By May 1903, a temporary tramway had been built to transport materials for the upper terminal. In early 1904 the ropeway was almost complete. The lower terminal was situated in West Dockyard next to what is today the Naval Museum, while the upper terminal was in the grounds of the sanatorium.

The ropeway was fitted with two wooden cages: one for conveying patients and staff, the other for stores and coal. The cage doors were wide enough to admit a stretcher, and inside was a seat and an electric control box. Cages were designed to stay on an even keel, with their centre of gravity below the point of suspension from the two-wheel carrier running along the wire.

Due to frequent bush fires, the wooden supports of the aerial ropeway were replaced by the present steel structures in 1913. Because of budget cuts and perceived inefficiency, the ropeway was shut down in 1927. The wire ropes were removed in 1934 and the cages used for timber. The lower-station waiting room can still be viewed at the Naval Museum as part of the museum collection.

CLOCK TOWER

British naval clock tower, sail loft and mast house

SA Naval Museum
West Dockyard
Simon's Town
Entrance on St George's Street
021-787-4686/4635
Daily 9am–3.30pm, except Good Friday, Christmas Day and New Year's Day
Free entry

Today, the old Royal Navy mast house is home to the SA Naval Museum. It's a fine building with an elegant clock tower. Few visitors to the museum realise that you can climb the stairs of the tower to the roof, where the beams are adorned with the names of British ships that

stopped in Simon's Town, such as HMS *Penelope* (1868), HMS *Blonde* (1889) and HMS *Barrosa* (1889).

A naval dockyard was established in Simon's Town by the Dutch in 1743. During the second occupation of the Cape by the British, which began in 1806, the Royal Navy also took up winter anchorage here.

When the Royal Navy's shore establishment moved from Cape Town to Simon's Town in 1814, construction of a handsome mast house was begun by royal engineers. It was completed the following year. The ground floor was used for the storage and repairing of boats, masts and spars. The upper floor was a sail loft for producing and storing sails. The mast house comprised a pair of linked, two-storey barns surmounted by a clock tower. The shape of the building was determined by the size of the masts, some of which were up to 36 metres in length. During its long history, the mast house has also been used as an Anglican chapel, a museum and as accommodation for sailors, especially during the First World War.

The clock itself has an interesting history. In an 1811 report, Simon's Town's deputy fiscal, Johannes Hendricus Brand, requested that a sundial be erected in the vicinity of the dockyard. This recommendation was improved upon by the installation of a clock in the mast-house tower.

The clock was manufactured by Thwaites and Reed of London, who first began making timepieces in 1740. The bells are dated 1816. The clock is of a posted-frame construction and incorporates three mechanisms: the gong (time), strike (hour bell) and chime (quarter-hour bell). Each mechanism is driven by a separate, manually-wound weight, the heaviest of which is about 180 kilograms.

This historic timepiece is one of the oldest public clocks in South Africa and still able to keep good time after two centuries of service – testament to the dedication of those who've tended it down the generations.

SAS *PRESIDENT KRUGER*
VESTIGES

Fragment of a doomed ship

Yard of the South African Naval Museum
Naval Dockyard
Simon's Town
Entrance on St George's Street opposite Arsenal Way
021-787-4686/4635
Daily 9am–3.30pm except Good Friday, Christmas Day and New Year's Day
Free entry

The SAS *President Kruger* was a frigate that sank in the South Atlantic after a collision with her replenishment ship, SAS *Tafelberg*. The tragic event took place 78 nautical miles southwest of Cape Point on 18 February 1982 and resulted in the loss of 16 lives. Due to the force of the impact, a section of the *President Kruger's* shipside plating was ripped off and embedded in the thicker steel of the bow of the *Tafelberg*. These two interlocking pieces of metal were removed when the *Tafelberg* was repaired and are now housed in the Naval Museum.

SAS *President Kruger* was one of three President-class frigates obtained from Britain by the South African Navy in the 1960s. At the time of the collision, the *Kruger* was conducting naval exercises with her sister ship, SAS *President Pretorius*, the submarine SAS *Emily Hobhouse* and the SAS *Tafelberg*. The exercises took place over several days with different candidate submarine captains being given the opportunity to mock-attack the *Tafelberg*. At night, the ships followed a zigzag course that allowed the submarine to continue engaging the ships in lower-intensity exercises while most of the crew rested.

At about 4am, the formation was ordered to reverse direction. The frigates had to turn first to maintain their protective positions ahead of the *Tafelberg*. Halfway through the turn, the operations room on *Kruger* lost contact with the *Tafelberg* in the radar 'clutter'. During an argument about the manoeuvre between the OOW (officer of the watch) and the PWO (principal warfare officer), the bows of the *Tafelberg* sliced into the *President Kruger's* port side. In a dramatic rescue operation conducted by the other two ships, 177 of Kruger's 193 crew were plucked from the icy waters.

A naval board of inquiry found a lack of seamanship by the captain and officers of the ship. A later inquest apportioned blame on the captain and PWO. However, none of the officers was court-martialled. Due to an international arms embargo against apartheid-era South Africa, the ship could not be replaced. Her loss was a crippling blow to the navy.

Cape Town's most loved dog

*Driving from Simon's Town over Red Hill on Red Hill Road (M66), turn left at
the 'Just Nuisance Grave 1.4 km' sign*

The only dog ever to be officially enlisted in the Royal Navy, Just Nuisance was a Great Dane that served at HMS *Afrikander*, a Simon's Town shore base, during World War II.

The grave lies among fynbos and sandstone outcrops in a quiet corner of the former South African Navy Signal School. A granite headstone reads: "Great Dane Just Nuisance, Able Seaman RN, HMS Afrikander, 1940–44, died 1 April 1944, age 7 years."

Nuisance was bought by Benjamin Chaney, who ran the United Services Institute in Simon's Town. The dog became popular with patrons of the institute, particularly the ratings, who took to feeding him nibbles and taking him for walks. The dog would follow them back to the naval base, where he would lounge on the decks of ships moored alongside. His preferred spot was at the top of the gangplank. Since he was a very large dog, even by Great Dane standards, he presented a considerable obstacle and became affectionately known as Nuisance.

The hound began taking day trips with the sailors by train to Cape Town. Despite the seamen's attempts to conceal him, conductors would eject him from the trains as soon as he was discovered. Railway officials even warned that he would have to be put down if he wasn't prevented from boarding trains.

The news that Nuisance was in serious trouble with the authorities prompted sailors and locals to write to the Navy, pleading that something be done. Naval command promptly enlisted the dog. As a member of the armed forces, Nuisance was now entitled to free rail travel. For the next few years he proved to be a morale booster for Simon's Town's military personnel.

In the enlistment papers, his surname was entered as 'Nuisance' and his forename 'Just'. His trade was listed as 'bone crusher' and his religious affiliation as 'scrounger', although this was subsequently amended to 'Canine Divinity League (Anti-Vivisection)'. Later, to allow him to receive rations and to reward him for long service, the dog was promoted from Ordinary Seaman to Able Seaman.

Upon his death, Just Nuisance was taken to Klaver Camp, where his body was draped with the Royal Navy's white ensign and buried with full naval honours, including a gun salute and the sounding of the 'Last Post'.

HERITAGE MUSEUM

The story of apartheid's forced evictions

Amlay House, King George's Way
Simon's Town
021-786-2302 or 082-257-5975
Sunday 10am–4pm or by appointment

The Heritage Museum is one of Cape Town's more characterful institutions. It lies just off St George's Street in the heart of Simon's Town and occupies the ground floor of Amlay House, built in 1858.

The building belonged to the Amlay family until they were forcibly removed when the town was declared a 'white area'. The heinous Group Areas Act was implemented by the Nationalist Government in 1967 and the Amlay family were among the last to leave, being evicted in 1975. They were also among the first former residents to return to Simon's Town in 1995.

The Heritage Museum was created as a reminder of the long trajectory of Muslim culture in the area, from the establishment of Simon's Town as official winter anchorage in 1743, until the forced removal of more than 7,000 'people of colour' under apartheid.

Displays include a large collection of old photographs and family trees, a traditional bridal room, handwritten kitab books, a traditional tea table and cooking utensils. There are also exhibits depicting aspects of Islamic culture at the Cape, including kramats (holy burial sites of notable sheikhs), religious artefacts and a pilgrimage room with displays of hajj attire. Most significant are the displays depicting forced removals, which bear witness to the trauma and loss during that dark period of Cape history.

Amlay House was owned by Councillor DA Amlay at the time of the removals. When the Land Restitution Programme was initiated after the end of apartheid, Amlay's daughter, Zainab (Patty) Davidson, submitted a claim for the properties her family had owned in Simon's Town. To her surprise, while they were awaiting the outcome of the claim, she received a call from the Department of Public Works. Patty was told that the navy had moved out of her childhood home and that it was standing vacant. She could rent it from the department at a nominal fee until the claim was settled. With seven bedrooms, the house was too big for Patty and her husband. So she struck upon the idea of establishing a museum, which opened in 1998. Family, friends and members of the community contributed photographs, newspaper clippings and oral histories, creating this important repository of memories.

MARTELLO TOWER

French-style fortification at the Cape

East Naval Dockyard
Simon's Town
021-787-4686/4635
To visit the tower, contact the SA Naval Museum (Warrant Officer Croome)
during office hours

The Martello Tower is a handsomely restored building that stands in the heart of the naval dockyard and harks back to a time when the British sought to defend the Cape against a French attack. The circular, stone tower has a lower level with a cannon display and an upper floor restored as guards' accommodation. The walls are nearly two metres thick and incorporate three large gun ports facing west.

When the British occupied the Cape in September 1795 they wanted to prevent any similar action by the French. The occupying troops were under the command of Major General James Craig, who

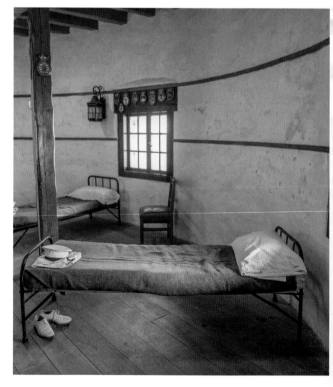

set about improving the coastal defences of Simon's Bay. He ordered the construction of a large powder magazine beside the harbour's southern battery. To protect the magazine, as well as the rear of the battery, he constructed a Martello tower in early 1796.

The History of Martello towers: from Mortella in France to Martello at the Cape

While engaged in blockading the French port of Toulon during the Napoleonic Wars, the British fleet needed a safe anchorage close by. On 8 February 1794 two British ships, *Fortitude* (74 guns) and *Juno* (32 guns), arrived to destroy the fortifications in Fiorenzo Bay, Corsica. At the western end of the bay, on Cape Mortella, stood a circular tower armed with two guns and a garrison of two grenadiers and 20 seamen.

During the attack, the small garrison put up such an effective defence that the severely damaged ships had to withdraw. Later, troops were put ashore and attacked the landward side of the fort. Victory was only achieved after the attacking troops managed to smoke out the defenders by setting fire to faggots piled against the tower. This remarkable achievement by such a small garrison immediately cemented the reputation of this type of fortification. Admiral Sir John Jervis aboard HMS *Victory* wrote: "I hope to see such works erected on every part of the coast likely for an enemy to make a descent on." The name 'Mortella' was corrupted to 'Martello' and dozens of such towers were subsequently built to defend British territory.

The Oldest Martello-Style Fort in the World

The Simon's Town tower is the oldest Martello-style fort in the world. Although it's modelled on the one in Corsica, it doesn't appear ever to have been mounted with sea-facing guns. Thus it was more of a blockhouse to protect the battery from landward attack than a 'true' Martello tower.

OLD BURYING GROUND

A cemetery for lost sailors

At the south end of Simon's Town
On the mountain side of Queens Road above Seaforth Beach
Entrances on Runciman Drive (best option) and Queens Road

Driving out of Simon's Town towards Cape Point, the Old Burying Ground is above the road on your right. This large, picturesque cemetery is surrounded by a stone wall and dotted with tall trees. The gravestones tell the history of Simon's Bay.

The Royal Navy transferred its headquarters to Simon's Town in 1814 and built a new hospital (now Hospital Terrace) for ill sailors. The town's growing population, as well as the arrival of a British Army contingent, necessitated a burial place and the present site above Seaforth Beach was chosen.

The Old Burying Ground was established circa 1814 and was initially used by local Anglicans. Dutch Reformed and Roman Catholic sections were added later. The Garden of Remembrance in the centre of the site was originally a naval cemetery under the care of the British War Graves Commission. It was later taken over by the National Monuments Council, which made a grant to the Simon's Town Municipality. The Dutch section was looked after by the Bloemfontein Boer War authorities.

The National Monuments Council ceased to exist in 1994 and care of the burying ground has been haphazard since; Simon's Town Historical Society does its best to maintain the site, mending boundary walls and repairing gravestones.

The oldest grave in the Garden of Remembrance is that of Rear Admiral Dundas (1775-1814). The most recent gravestones are from HMS *Birkenhead*, which struck the rocks off Danger Point near Cape Agulhas on 26 February 1852.

Keep your eye out for the graves of 20 sailors off HMS *Glendower*. They were drowned when the pinnace carrying them back to their ship from West Dockyard capsized in stormy weather on 10 March 1826.

There are about 550 sailors, marines, soldiers and 50 Kroomen (African sailors, mostly from Ivory Coast and Liberia, recruited into the Royal Navy) buried in the Garden of Remembrance. It's sobering to see how young many of the sailors were – some less than 15 years old.

During the Anglo-Boer War of 1899-1902, many Boer POWs were detained in Simon's Town. Sick prisoners were cared for in the nearby Palace Barracks Hospital, where the famous author Mary Kingsley served as one of the nurses (she contracted typhoid and died here on 3 June 1900). More than 160 prisoners perished – some from wounds, but most of them from typhoid and measles. Look out for the war memorial to 82 Boer combatants buried in the cemetery.

ALBATROSS ROCK

23

Shipwrecks of a treacherous rock

Shipwreck Trail
Cape Point section of Table Mountain National Park
021-780-9204
Map at Buffelsfontein Visitors' Centre

Hidden beneath the water off Olifantsbos Point lies Albatross Rock. In heavy seas you can see waves breaking over this ship trap, which lies about 1.5 kilometres offshore. This dangerous rock has caused the demise of half a dozen ships.

Evidence of its destructive power can be viewed along the Shipwreck Trail. Substantial pieces of the *Thomas T Tucker,* including iron ribs and bollards, were washed up at Olifantsbos. Most of the wreckage is on the rocks and among the pools south of the point (best viewed at low tide) but you'll also find bits of wreckage strewn along the beach.

The *Thomas T Tucker* struck Albatross Rock on 27 November 1942. She was a liberty ship, one of nearly 3,000 similar vessels constructed in the United States during World War II. These ships served as armed merchantmen, carrying war material and food supplies to the Allies.

The *Thomas T Tucker* left New Orleans on her maiden voyage, bound for North Africa via the Cape. She carried supplies and Sherman tanks for the Allied armies ranged against Rommel's Axis forces in the Western Desert.

The waters off the Cape were patrolled by German submarines at the time, but it was not a U-boat's torpedo that holed her. Rather, it was foul weather and human error that caused the *Tucker* to run ashore at Olifantsbos. The coaster *Swazi* went alongside to take off her valuable cargo and a ferricrete road was constructed to allow other material to be removed by land.

The first recorded victim of the rock was the steam-tug *Albatross*, which gave the maritime hazard its name. En route from Simon's Town to Table Bay with a cargo of cotton, she struck the blinder in 1863.

The rock's second victim was the steamer RMS *Kafir*, wrecked south of Olifantsbos after striking Albatross in 1878. Just two years later, the barque *Star of Africa*, locally owned and bound for Cape Town from Calcutta, fell foul of the dangerous rock.

Another local coaster, the SS *Umhlali*, was next in 1909, followed in 1917 by the Swedish freighter *Bia*. The last vessel to succumb to the rock was the Dutch coaster *Nolloth*, wrecked here in rough seas in 1965. Pieces of the *Nol-loth* still litter the beach south of Olifantsbos, close to the remains of the *Thomas T Tucker*.

PAULSBERG CANNON

24

A 'Napoleonic radar'

The cannon is a 45-minute walk up the path behind Bordjies Rif parking lot along the Farmer's Cliff Trail in Cape Point Nature Reserve

On top of Paulsberg, on the eastern seaboard of Cape Point Nature Reserve, stands a Dutch 4-pounder cannon. Painted black, it sits in a commanding position with uninterrupted views of the Atlantic Ocean, Cape Point and False Bay. Until recently, the gun's purpose remained something of a mystery.

From a military perspective, a small, single gun could not have served any defensive purpose, as it did not cover any significant access routes to the Cape's settlements; nor could it have inflicted any damage on passing ships.

However, the naval presence in Simon's Town necessitated some form of warning system should an enemy ship enter False Bay and threaten the anchorage. For this reason, both the Dutch and later the English had established gun batteries in Simon's Town. Paulsberg cannon was, in all likelihood, a signal cannon – the first cog in an early warning system that stretched up the west coast of False Bay.

Jim Hallinan, former social ecologist for the Cape Peninsula National Park, set about solving the riddle of the Paulsberg gun. He unearthed archival documents that presented important clues. A number of early 19th-century letters tell us that the signal post was permanently manned, even in peacetime. This suggests that the gun transmitted signals other than purely warning ones, perhaps to advise the colony of arriving ships.

From letters between Mr Bird, Acting Colonial Secretary, and Mr PS Buissine, Deputy Fiscal, we can determine with certainty that signalling was conducted from Paulsberg, and that the adjacent hut was already in disrepair by 1809, only the third year of English occupation. This suggests that the gun was probably used by the Dutch prior to the invasion of the English in 1806. Further letters note that Paulsberg was the "foremost signal post," meaning that the signal travelled in a northerly direction via other similar posts.

The absence of noise pollution in 1809 meant that in favourable weather conditions (such as a cold day with low cloud and a following wind) the sound of a 4-pounder firing a blank charge could be heard for about eight kilometres. A reasonable expectation would be for the sound to carry six kilometres. We can thus assume that there would have been about three other posts between Paulsberg and the naval station at Simon's Town. In other words, this was Napoleonic radar.

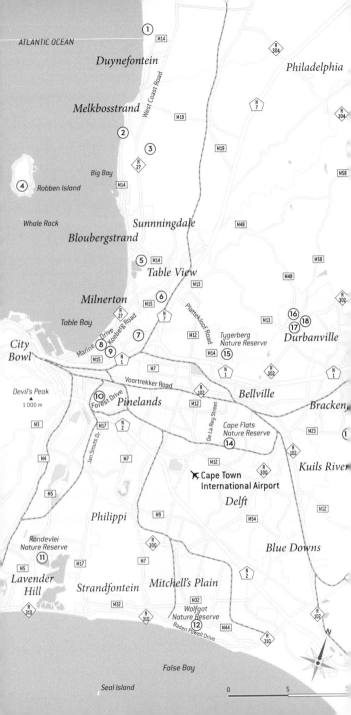

West Coast & Cape Flats

KOEBERG NATURE RESERVE

Mountain biking with eland around a nuclear power station

Approximately 30km north of Cape Town off the R27
Daily between sunrise and sunset
Entry free, but bring identification for gate security

A frica's only nuclear power plant seems an unlikely place to go for a spot of mountain biking or a relaxing walk along the beach. However, Koeberg Power Station, just 30km from central Cape Town, is surrounded by a 3,000-hectare nature reserve, complete with herds of eland, zebra, gemsbok and springbok, as well as more than 170 species of birds, all thriving in the rare and threatened West Coast strandveld.

Koeberg Nature Reserve is the property of South Africa's national electricity supplier, Eskom. It was established in 1991 (six years after the construction of the power station was completed) as part of Eskom's environmental policy and serves as an outdoor education centre for the community. Koeberg encourages visitors to explore the reserve via two walking trails and a mountain-bike trail.

All trails start from the visitors' parking lot, where there is an information kiosk providing pamphlets and a map. The shorter Grysbok Trail (either 2.5km or 5.7km) follows a circular route around wetlands to a viewpoint of Table Mountain from the beach. The Dikkop Trail, heading towards the opposite end of the reserve, is a series of interconnected paths, including a 2km stretch along the beach. These paths can be walked as a 9.5km, 19.3km or 22.3km circular trail, depending on your time and energy. Pack a picnic lunch and enjoy it on the beach.

For mountain bikers, there is a well-marked 19km trail with three loops. The route is fairly flat and on well-maintained 4x4 tracks, making it a good outing for the less fit or for families with children. The furthest section of the trail leads cyclists to a bird hide where there are good chances of spotting pelicans, flamingos and fish eagles. For a few extra kilometres (and some sand riding) it's worth taking the right turn down to the beach on the way back. Look out for the lone eland; one cyclist returned rather breathless to say he'd been chased halfway around the reserve by it. According to Eskom's environmental officer, the eland was probably just lonely and looking for company.

Lucky visitors may also spot some of the small predators in the reserve, which include the African wild cat, genet and caracal (rooikat). The best time to visit is in spring (August to September) when a spectacular display of wild flowers carpets the reserve. Remember to pack sunblock and a hat, as there's no shade in the reserve.

HAAKGAT POINT

The most extreme windsurfing in town

3km north of Blouberg and 1km south of Melkbosstrand on Otto du Plessis Drive (M14)
Look out for the sign and small parking lot on the sea side of the road

Haakgat is arguably the most radical windsurfing and kitesurfing beach in Cape Town. It's a fickle spot that only works with the right southeasterly wind and large southwesterly swell conditions. But when it fires and the message does the rounds of the local surfing community, the wave riding and jumping here are spectacular to watch.

Cape Town is a world-class destination for kitesurfing and windsurfing. During the summer months, foreign wave riders, particulary from Europe, descend on local beaches, armed to the teeth with boards, sails and kites.

The most popular spots are Sunset Beach, Kite Beach (Table View) and Big Bay (Blouberg). However, the less frequented and less well-known Haakgat provides the most extreme sailing. It's here that you'll see the best wave riders pulling the most radical maneuvers. On quiet days the beach is also pretty good for angling and fly fishing.

Haakgat is a left-hand point break located across the road from the

Atlantic Beach Golf Club. You'll know straight away if it's a good day by the line of cars parked along Otto du Plessis Drive near the entrance to the small parking lot. Due to the number of Italian windsurfers who frequent Haakgat, it's sometimes known as Little Italy.

The waves here can get enormous and still hold their shape, giving a long, clean ride when the wind is side-shore (it's best at high tide). Sometimes the break is very hollow and creates ramps for aerial maneuvers. In perfect conditions, sailors can surf the wave for more than 200 metres.

However, the shorebreak can be treacherous and there are strong rip currents close to the beach. The rocks can also make for a sticky landing. In short, Haakgat is only for advanced wave riders, especially at high tide and when there are big waves.

Rietvlei Flat-Water Sailing

For beginners, there's a lake with good conditions just behind the sand dunes at Sunset Beach. Rietvlei is also a stretch of water where sailors can test new equipment, take part in races or practice flat-water speed sailing in a safe, confined environment. The launching spot is at Milnerton Aquatic Club on the vlei's eastern shore.

BLAAUWBERG HILL & RADAR STATION

A small but significant contribution to naval defence during WWII

Access only by booking accommodation or on guided walks with the Friends of the BCA
021-444-0454
For accommodation, reservations.blaauwberg@capetown.gov.za or for guided walks, chair@bca.org.za
bca.org.za

F ew people know that Blaauwberg Hill played a part in the Allied effort in World War II. The hill, now part of Blaauwberg Nature Reserve, was the site of a radar station during the conflict. The old bunker affords stunning views of Robben Island, Melkbos and Koeberg to the north, and Table Mountain to the south. Lining its walls are maps of the old radar stations of the Cape Peninsula and lists of ships sunk

in the area. Although it is camouflaged by an undulating silhouette and sand-coloured surface, the building is visible from the R27 coast road.

During the war, the Cape was a major route between west and east for ships carrying troops and supplies. Around 18,000 ships called at Cape Town between 1939 and 1945. In the same period 156 Allied ships were sunk within 1,600 kilometres of the coast of the Union of South Africa. German, Italian and Japanese submarines accounted for 134 of these (of which only one was a warship). It's thought that the number would have been much higher, however, were it not for the Cape's secret radar stations operated by the SSS – the Special Signals Services.

The radar stations, usually in isolated and elevated locations, beamed radio pulses across the sea. Any vessel or aircraft within range of these pulses would reflect them, appearing as 'blips' on a screen. The radar operators at Blaauwberg – mostly women – were trained to differentiate between these blips and had to determine whether they were, for example, fishing boats or enemy submarines.

Information about suspicious craft was then sent to the Combined Operations centre at the Castle, where it would be decided whether to dispatch a South African Air Force aircraft to investigate, and drop depth charges if necessary. Radar was also used to help friendly ships avoid the treacherous shoreline of the Cape, as no lighthouses were functioning at the time and there was an enforced 'wireless silence'. Apparently, the Cape's 'hush-hush' radar stations were guarded by men with assegais, to prevent enemy spies from discovering their location and purpose.

 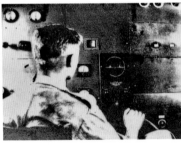

A World War II officers' mess building just a few steps away from the radar station was recently renovated and converted into self-catering accommodation. It was named after the *Scelotes montispectus*, a new species of burrowing skink discovered in the reserve in 2002 and thought to be found only here. Montispectus means 'to behold the mountain' – Blaauwberg Hill certainly offers superlative views of Table Mountain.

ROBBEN ISLAND'S 9-INCH GUNS

Defending Cape Town with heavy artillery

Western shore of Robben Island
Visit the battery while on an island tour (ask your guide for it to be included)

Most visitors to Robben Island focus on the famous prison and Mandela's cell, but the island also has a fascinating World War II history. Of nearly a hundred 9.2-inch guns that did service worldwide during the war, only about 28 remain. Of these, 12 are in South Africa. The Number 3 gun of De Waal Battery is the only gun in the world that has been restored as a moving display. Ask your island guide for it to be included, as it's sometimes missed out on the official tour.

With the outbreak of World War II, Robben Island became the nucleus of the Cape Peninsula's coastal defence system. The Suez Canal was vulnerable to attack by the Germans and shipping traffic in South African waters was expected to increase dramatically. By 1942, the Mediterranean had become a battleground, and huge convoys carrying reinforcements and war materiel rounded the Cape in a constant stream. Between 1941 and 1944, almost 50,000 ships visited South African harbours.

Given the absence of a large naval force, fixed coastal defences were crucial and Robben Island became a stationary battleship in Table Bay. It was decided that a high-angle, 9.2-inch gun battery would provide the best long-range defence. Combined with the powerful batteries at Simon's Town and Llandudno, the three sets of guns were designed to support each other, their arcs of fire overlapping to cover the coastline and the peninsula's harbours.

Fortification of the island involved bringing 150,000 tons of equipment and materiel, building roads, a harbour, underground magazines and watch towers as well as accommodation for thousands, recreational facilities and a runway.

The 9.2-inch gun emplacements also needed ancillary points, such as observation posts, a power station, plotting rooms and magazines. Most of these were dug up to 10 metres underground. In addition, the island's perimeter was fortified with machine-gun posts, searchlight stations and barbed-wire barriers, especially after the attack on Pearl Harbour and the resultant fear of a Japanese invasion.

Manufactured by the Royal Gun Factory at Woolwich, London, in 1901, De Waal Battery's Number 3 gun arrived in the Cape in November 1940. The gun weighs 140 tons and had a range of almost 30km. The official opening of the restored gun took place on 4 March 2011. It's now a moving display (rarely on show to the public), with all the hydraulics working, enabling the turret to be traversed through 360° and the gun elevated 25°. Even the loading/ramming mechanism is operational once again.

SANCCOB

The extraordinary endeavour to save the African penguin

22 Pentz Drive, Table View
sanccob.co.za
Monday–Friday, tours at 11am and 3pm; every second Saturday at 10am, 12 noon and 3pm
Tours must be booked in advance

While locals and tourists alike delight in the antics of the African penguins at Boulders Beach, they're usually unaware that most of the important work being done to save these endangered seabirds goes on at a rescue centre on the other side of the city. SANCCOB (the Southern African Foundation for the Conservation of Coastal Birds) on the northern end of Table Bay is one of only a handful of marine-bird rescue centres worldwide.

When a tanker sank off the coast of Cape Town on 23 June 2000, spilling 1,300 tonnes of fuel, SANCCOB mobilised the world's largest animal rescue effort, saving the lives of 40,000 penguins and other birds. Even in a year with no oil spills, SANCCOB treats about 2,500 injured, oiled or ill seabirds and abandoned chicks. Most of these birds are African penguins, but they also treat cormorants and gulls.

If you love penguins and are interested in learning more about them, a one-hour 'behind the scenes' tour of SANCCOB will give you a glimpse into the activities of this busy seabird hospital. You'll get to see the birds being washed, cared for and fed. You'll also get to meet one of the penguin ambassadors, which include Rocky the rock-hopper penguin and Skipper the African penguin.

At the chick-rearing unit, abandoned eggs and chicks are reared and released back into the wild. More than 2,000 chicks have been successfully released since the unit opened in 2011. Visitors view the hatching and chick-rearing rooms through a window to ensure that diseases aren't introduced. Interestingly, research has found that hand-raised chicks are more likely than wild-reared chicks to survive to breeding age; they also breed more than other birds.

SANCCOB is a nonprofit organisation and relies on donations and volunteers. Visit their website www.sanccob.co.za to find out how you can help.

NEARBY
The Rietvlei Wetland Reserve
Daily 7.30am–5pm

Just around the corner, at 10 Sandpiper Crescent, is the entrance to one of Cape Town's most important areas for waterbirds. Rietvlei is a 560-hectare freshwater wetland on the floodplain of the Diep River. Thanks to a variety of wetland habitats and its proximity to the ocean, more than 100 species of waterbird have been recorded here, including kingfishers, teals, herons, grebes, terns and cormorants, as well as both greater and lesser flamingos and great white pelicans. Rietvlei is part of the Table Bay Nature Reserve.

MA TZU TEMPLE

A privately-funded Taiwanese temple for fishermen

5A Illy Industrial Park, Stella Road, Montagu Gardens
Daily 9.30am–4.30pm

In Montagu Gardens, hidden away in a concrete bungalow in the middle of an industrial park, is a Taiwanese temple dedicated to the goddess Ma Tzu. The Taoist patron goddess of seafarers, Ma Tzu (also spelt Mazu and Matsu), is the deity most commonly worshipped by Taiwanese islanders.

According to legend, Ma Tzu (meaning 'mother-ancestor') was born on 23 March in the year 960 during the Song Dynasty. She was the seventh daughter of a fisherman's family. Stories about her vary, but all agree that she would stand on the shore in a red dress to guide fishing boats home. Ma Tzu has become an important figure for overseas Chinese and Taiwanese around the world.

Cape Town harbour is one of the most significant ports of call for Taiwanese fishing fleets. Crew members come here to pray, give thanks

for her blessing and protection, and to ask for guidance. The temple is privately funded by the local Taiwanese community but visitors of all cultures are welcome. Special activities are held for Ma Tzu's birthday festival in March each year.

When you visit, walk through the antechamber into the central room and take four incense sticks (you can place a donation in the red box). Light them and then go back into the antechamber and pray to heaven. Put one stick of incense into the big bowl in the antechamber, place fruit or a gift on the large table in the main room then go to the front altar to pray to Ma Tzu (the central figure), placing another incense stick in front of her. Move right to pray to Tai Suey and place a third stick of incense in that bowl. Lastly, go back into the antechamber to pray to the Five Tiger Generals, who represent the earth.

To find out what your future holds, go again to the altar of Ma Tzu and pray for guidance to formulate your question. Then draw a stick from the oracle bowl and throw the two rounded wooden pieces next to the bowl: if one flat side faces up and the other down, you have the correct stick. Take the stick to Mr Hong, the temple's priest, who will interpret its meaning for you.

INTAKA ISLAND

A birder's heaven in the centre of a new city

Park Way, Century City
October-April daily 7.30am–7pm
May–September daily 7.30am–5.30pm

Many Capetonians view Century City as an unattractive 'Johannesburg by the Sea', yet even those living next door to the Western Cape's largest shopping mall and business park are unaware that at its centre is a beautiful and valuable wetland reserve. The 16-hectare nature area is home to more than 200 species of indigenous plants and 120 bird species, as well as important breeding heronries for water birds.

Before the property developers arrived, the land was covered in thick alien vegetation, and the large wetland area hidden within was only found during an aerial survey. Those birders lucky enough to have heard of its discovery had to battle through thickets of invasive Port Jackson to reach it. But when they did, they were amazed at how unspoilt this little gem of a wetland was.

When the development of Century City started in the mid-1990s, nature lovers who knew of the wetland's existence were dismayed, assuming it would be destroyed. However, the Century City developers chose to preserve it and created the Intaka Island wetland reserve.

Intaka (which means 'bird' in Xhosa) began as a simple, low-budget affair, but today is one of the best-run wetland reserves in South Africa. Maintenance of the wetlands is kept as natural and eco-friendly as possible. A system of four 'cells' in the wetlands uses reeds, wind and shallow water to filter and aerate the water that flows in from the canals around Century City.

There are three perennial ponds forming the 'constructed' wetlands, while the eastern side of the reserve is taken up by a seasonal pan that has been left largely untouched. The pan fills with water during winter and slowly dries up during summer, leaving an accumulation of salt. This pan, surrounded by Cape Flats sand fynbos and strandveld, is representative of how most of the Cape Flats would have looked 200 years ago.

Among those people in on the secret of Intaka Island are keen bird photographers. At sunrise, they flock to a hide located just a few feet from kingfisher perches to get fantastic close-ups of malachite and pied kingfishers. Other birds you are likely to see include a variety of herons, African spoonbills, red-knobbed coots, dabchicks, red bishops, weavers, moorhens and mallards.

Visitors can stroll along the self-guided footpaths (there are two short, circular trails) or be shown around by a field ranger. Alternatively, you can take a boat ride around the island on the Century City ferry.

KLEIN ZOAR HOUSE

The home of a South African hero

4 Wemyss Street, Brooklyn
Private home

Declared a national monument in 1971, Klein Zoar House is a simple, thatched house that dates from the early 18th century and is thought to have been the home of a South African hero, Wolraad Woltemade.

There are very few surviving examples of three-century-old Cape cottages and this is a particularly fine one. It's a private home, tucked behind foliage at the end of Wemyss Street beside Zoar Vlei, the last remnant of Paarden Eiland's former wetlands.

On 1 June 1773 the *Jonge Thomas*, a Dutch East India ship, was anchored near the mouth of the Salt River. In the early hours of the morning, the storm that had been raging through the night intensified. The ship's captain, Barend Lameren, ordered that a cannon be fired to warn people on shore that they may need help.

Just before dawn the *Jonge Thomas* broke loose from her anchor and hit a sandbar off the river mouth. Lives were lost as the ship began breaking up, but many survivors clung to the wreck. The stricken ship was not far from land and some sailors tried to swim for shore; most drowned in the attempt.

A crowd of onlookers gathered on the beach, attended by a detachment of soldiers to keep order. Corporal Christian Ludwig Wol-

temade, the youngest son of the elderly Wolraad, was among those standing guard. As daylight came, Wolraad left his home on horseback, carrying provisions for his son.

Shocked to see that nothing was being done by those on the beach, Wolraad rode his horse Vonk (Spark) into the sea to attempt a rescue. Approaching the wreck, Woltemade called for two men to jump into the water and grasp the horse's tail, dragging them to shore.

Wolraad went back again and again, rescuing 14 men in total. By now, horse and rider were exhausted. Suddenly, the ship began to sink. Wolraad once more urged his horse into the waves. Seeing this was their last chance at escape, six men dived into the water, grabbing the horse. Their weight was too great and all were dragged under and drowned.

Woltemade became an instant hero. The Dutch East India Company (VOC) provided for his widow and children and named a ship, *De Held Woltemade*, after him. His name was later given to the SA *Wolraad Woltemade*, a powerful salvage tug built in 1976. In 1970 the Woltemade Decoration for Bravery was instituted as the highest civilian honour for courage in South Africa.

SOUTH AFRICAN AIR FORCE MUSEUM

The home of legendary aircraft

The entrance to Ysterplaat Air Force Base is at the end of Piet Grobler Street, Brooklyn
The museum is inside the base
021-508-6576
Wednesday–Friday 7am–3pm; Saturday 8am–12.30pm
Free entry

The South African Air Force (SAAF) Museum at Ysterplaat is dedicated to the history of military aviation. It has a wide variety of exhibits covering the period of the SAAF's existence since its inception in 1920. In addition to aircraft, models, weapons, engines and uniforms, there's also a display of Royal Flying Corps memorabilia. The museum's most important exhibits are its historic aircraft, some of which are still in working order.

The SAAF Museum is maintained by a group of aviation enthusiasts. Displays focus on South Africa's involvement in World War II, the Berlin Blockade, Korean War and Bush War. There's also an exhibition of women in aviation and a detailed history of Ysterplaat. Look out for the small planetarium used for training cadet pilots to navigate without instruments or GPS.

The museum has a gift shop selling books, models and posters, as well as a library with a selection of aviation-related publications, research material, logbooks and photographs.

Vintage planes are kept in the museum's hangar, as well as in Hangar Four, which lies inside the high-security section of the base (only open to the public on Saturday mornings, or by appointment). Aircraft on show include a Ventura, a Dakota and Mirages.

The First Jet to Cross the Atlantic

Perhaps the two most interesting aircraft on display are the De Havilland Vampire (in the museum hangar) and Avro Shackleton Mark 3 (in Hangar Four).

The Vampire was a British jet fighter developed during World War II. It entered service with the Royal Air Force in 1945 but was too late to see action. However, it did record several aviation milestones, including being the first jet to cross the Atlantic. Vampires were assembled at Ysterplaat and became the SAAF's first operational jet fighters. A total of 77 were delivered to South Africa.

Ysterplaat is also home to the last airworthy Shackleton (a British-made, long-range maritime patrol aircraft). The plane has been grounded as there are not enough qualified aircrew to operate it. Shackletons were flown from Ysterplaat by 35 Squadron between 1957 and 1984. Missions were mostly patrols of the sea lanes around the Cape, but some occasionally ranged as far as Antarctica.

STROLL AROUND CENTRAL SQUARE

The green centre of South Africa's first garden city

In the middle of Pinelands at the intersection of Broad Walk, Central Avenue and St Stephen's Road

Central Square in Pinelands is the heart of a 'garden city' that harks back to a mid-20th-century, Anglicised Cape Town, reminiscent of similar, planned suburbs in England, such as Milton Keynes.

The garden-city movement is a philosophy of urban planning conceived in 1898 by Sir Ebenezer Howard in the UK. New urban centres were designed as self-contained communities ringed by green-belts containing mixed zones of housing, industry and agriculture. The idea was for spacious, well-planned suburbs with sports facilities, amenities and good traffic flow.

Richard Stuttaford, of the well-known Cape Town merchant family, started the Garden Cities Trust in 1918. The suburb of Pinelands was designed in Britain and became South Africa's first garden city.

Start your stroll on the square's west side, where Broad Walk enters Central Square. In front of you lies the suburb's founding stone, laid by General Jan Smuts on 5 May 1923. Walking anti-clockwise, you'll pass an old red cannon, excavated during the building work. On the northeast side of the square stands the memorial gateway, constructed in 1960 to honour those who fell during World War II.

A commemorative stone on the western side of the square is dedicated to the ship's company of HMSAS *Southern Floe*, sunk by a mine in 1941. In December 1940 four South African anti-submarine vessels were sent to the Mediterranean to help combat the Axis forces. The ships were involved in operations from a base in Alexandria but later moved to Tobruk in Libya. On 11 February 1941, HMSAS *Southern Floe* was blown up close to Tobruk harbour. She was the first South African Naval Forces casualty in the Second World War.

Of the 28-man crew, only Leading Stoker C Jones survived. He'd joined the ship shortly before she sailed from Alexandria, having been lent to *Southern Floe* by HMS *Gloucester*. After the war, Jones continued to place a memorial notice in Cape Town newspapers until he too passed away.

At the northern corner of the square stands St Stephen's Anglican Church, which has a garden of remembrance and a lovely chapel tucked away behind the main building. This quaint, thatched chapel was constructed in 1926 and opened by South Africa's governor general, the Earl of Athlone.

THE RUNAWAY HIPPOS OF RONDEVLEI

Cape Town's only population of hippopotami

Rondevlei Nature Reserve, Fisherman's Walk, Grassy Park
imvubu.co.za
Daily 7.30am–5pm and 7.30am–7pm on Saturdays and Sundays from December to February

Hidden in the centre of the none too salubrious suburbs of Grassy Park, Zeekoevlei and Lavender Hill, is the 290-hectare wetland of Rondevlei Nature Reserve. The large, brackish lagoon is home to about 280 indigenous plant species, 230 species of birds, a variety of reptiles and small mammals, and the only hippopotamus population in Cape Town.

Hippos were once plentiful on the Cape Peninsula. Just 18 days after Jan van Riebeeck landed at the Cape in 1652, his men shot a hippo near what is now Church Square in central Cape Town. They soon discovered that hippo meat is tasty and their skin makes excellent whips and rope. By the 1700s, all the hippos in the Western Cape had been hunted. Then, in 1981, two male hippos were relocated from KwaZulu-Natal to try to control an invasive South American grass smothering the wetland. They were joined three years later by two females and in August 1984 the first baby hippo in nearly 300 years was born at Rondevlei. Today there are about six hippos living in the reserve. They help to maintain the wetland's biodiversity and have played an important role in re-establishing hippos in other Western Cape conservation areas. They also have a reputation for escaping.

The escapees are usually young males forced out by the dominant bull. The first escape occurred in February 2004 when a calf named Houdini made off into the Zeekoevlei river after thieves broke the fence. Houdini stayed on the run for 10 months, grazing on garden lawns, until he was caught after a chaotic three-and-a-half-hour chase and sent to a private reserve in the Eastern Cape. In 2009 a four-year-old hippo, nicknamed Zorro because of his zigzag scar, got out and lived in the adjacent sewerage works for 18 months before being sent to a reserve in Worcester. And in August 2012 a cow and her calf, followed by a young bull, wandered out of the reserve when a section of fencing was stolen.

As hippos tend to stay underwater during the day, your best chance of spotting one is to arrive as early as possible in the morning or late in the afternoon. Take a stroll with your binoculars around the one-kilometre waterside trail that leads past six bird hides and two observation towers. For a better chance of seeing the hippos, contact Imvubu Island, which runs an overnight bush camp on a small island in the reserve as well as chartered boat trips.

WOLFGAT NATURE RESERVE

Ancient home of the brown hyena

On both sides of Baden Powell Drive, Mitchell's Plain, between the Mnandi and Monwabisi recreation resorts
021-392-5134/5

Wolfgat is a small, unfenced nature reserve on the False Bay coast. It boasts stunning views from the cliffs and dunes, taking in the entire shoreline from Cape Hangklip to Cape Point.

This conservation area comprises 248 hectares of endangered flora and limestone cliffs. The reserve protects coastal fynbos and Cape Flats dune strandveld vegetation types (only 32% of their original range is left in greater Cape Town). Plant species include evergreen shrubs, flowering succulents, arum lilies and varieties of daisies. Birds such as kelp gulls and African oystercatchers also nest here.

A major threat to the reserve is the invasive alien Acacia cyclops (or rooikrans). This 'weed' has spread across large sections of the coastline and flats, smothering local vegetation and disturbing coastal ecosystems.

Activities for visitors include picnicking, nature walks, fishing in designated areas (permit required), bird watching, whale watching, swimming and paragliding.

The reserve's custodians, working in partnership with many organisations and individuals, aim to protect this community asset for the benefit of those living in the adjacent areas of Mitchell's Plain and Khayelitsha. In addition, school children and university students use the reserve as a learning and research environment.

Cape Town is unique among world cities due to its high concentration of flora and fauna found within its boundaries. Wolfgat Nature Reserve is managed by the City of Cape Town in partnership with the local communities of Khayelitsha and Mitchell's Plain.

As this is an isolated, unfenced area, for your own safety it's best to visit Wolfgat in a group. And don't carry any valuables.

The name 'Wolfgat' means 'Wolf's Cave' and refers to the brown hyena or strandwolf, which roamed the area until the 19th century. A fossilised den was found here in the 1960s and this stretch of coast was named after the discovery.

MARVOL MUSEUM

A little piece of Russia in wine country

Hazendal Estate, Kuilsriver
021-903-5035
Driving towards Stellenbosch on La Belle Road (M31), turn left onto Bottelary
Road (M23); the Hazendal entrance is on the left after three sets of traffic lights
Daily 10am–4pm

Marvol is a curious and incongruous museum that houses Russian art and artefacts on an old Cape wine estate. The downstairs section displays a selection of Fabergé eggs and a range of Russian religious

icons portraying the saints, disciples, Virgin and Jesus. The upper storey is devoted to a collection of *matryoshka* dolls and realist paintings depicting typical Russian pastoral scenes, snow-covered landscapes and towns.

The museum is the brainchild of Mark Voloshin, one of the Russian owners of Hazendal Estate, a wine farm founded in 1699. When he first arrived in South Africa, Voloshin was often asked about his heritage. The Marvol Museum of Russian Art and Culture is his response to that interest.

Voloshin was born in Moscow, studied dentistry at the Moscow Medical Dental Institute and later turned to business, becoming a founder of the Marvol Group, with interests in manufacturing, trade, finance, marketing and consulting. In 1994 he and his business partner purchased Hazendal Estate. The old farm buildings were restored and a museum created to showcase Voloshin's private collection of eclectic art and artefacts.

Fabergé eggs are a feature of the museum. Hand-crafted by Peter Carl Fabergé, such eggs were first created as an Easter gift from Tsar Alexander III to his wife. This trend carried on long after the tsar's death, with Fabergé perfecting the art of fashioning exquisite jewelled eggs.

Many Russian Fabergé eggs and imperial artworks were destroyed or sold after the revolution in 1917. Under Voloshin's direction, a set of modern Fabergé eggs was made and presented to President Nelson Mandela in 1997. Some of them were auctioned to raise money for the Nelson Mandela Children's Fund. The remaining eggs are on display in the museum.

While on Hazendal you can do some wine tasting, enjoy a meal at the farm's Hermitage Restaurant or picnic on the lawns with fine views of the farm buildings and vineyards beyond.

CAPE FLATS NATURE RESERVE

A last fragment of the original Cape Flats floral kingdom

University of the Western Cape, Robert Sobukwe Road, Belville
Monday–Friday 9am–5pm
Free entry

A dusty, windblown corner of southern Belville is hardly the place you'd expect to find an ecological treasure. But at the entrance to the campus of the University of the Western Cape (UWC) is a tiny nature reserve that protects one of the last fragments of Cape Flats sand fynbos.

Once, the Cape Flats boasted one of the highest rates of floral diversity in the world, but now, as a result of urbanisation and an almost complete lack of conservation, the area has the unfortunate distinction of producing the world's highest rate of plant extinction.

Established in 1977, the Cape Flats Nature Reserve was created as a refuge for Cape Flats sand fynbos and Cape Flats dune strandveld. The reserve was made a national monument the following year. It's a private reserve, administered by the university, which uses it as a base for ecological and environmental education and research.

More than 220 indigenous plant species have been identified here, several of which are endemic to the reserve, meaning they are found nowhere else on earth. Plant types include sedges, grasses, geophytes, reeds, succulents, and a wealth of spring annuals, such as the Cape rain daisy (*Dimorphotheca pluvialis*) and the hongerblom (*Senecio littoreus*), which form carpets of white and yellow blossoms on the dunes between August and September.

More than 80 bird species have been recorded in the reserve and a bird hide overlooks a small wetland supporting waterfowl and waders such as Cape teal and blacksmith lapwing. There are a few small mammals and at least one reclusive caracal (lynx). You may be lucky enough to spot grysbok, grey mongoose or Cape hare. There is also the chance of seeing Cape cobra, angulate tortoise, Cape dwarf chameleon and the sand rain frog. Interestingly, the tiny black percher dragonfly (*Diplacodes lefebrvii*), which had never before been recorded on the Cape Peninsula, was spotted here for the first time in March 2014.

The reserve also maintains an excellent nursery where indigenous and rare Cape Flats plants are raised. As the reserve unit's ultimate objective is not just to preserve this small corner, but also to try to expand the shrinking Cape Flats ecosystem, the plants are available for sale to visitors at extremely affordable prices – some for as little as R5. In this way, the reserve hopes to make gardening with indigenous plants more common, particularly in the surrounding neighbourhoods.

TYGERBERG NATURE RESERVE

A last vestige of urban renosterveld

Main gate on Totius Street, Welgemoed
Secondary gate on Meyboom Avenue, Plattekloof
021-444-8971
Monday–Friday 7.30am–6pm, weekends 7.30am–7pm

Tygerberg Nature Reserve was established in 1973 to protect one of the last remnants of critically endangered Swartland shale renosterveld vegetation. This veld type is named after the rhinos that once roamed the area. The reserve covers 309 hectares and boasts 562 plant species. Of these, 23 are threatened, eight are endemic to Cape Town and three endemic to Tygerberg itself.

Just inside the main gate is the Kristo Pienaar Environmental Education Centre with conservation displays, as well as an aromatic and medicinal garden. As you ascend the hill, the path splits into a number of walking trails, ranging from a few hundred metres to more than three kilometres. There are also two attractive picnic sites and a wheelchair route.

The views from the summit of Tygerberg Hill take in the sweep of the Cape Flats, from the Hottentot's Holland Mountains to Table Mountain and both False and Table Bays. The eastern slope of the reserve consists of old ploughed fields that are in the process of being restored, while the western slope is close to being pristine Swartland shale renosterveld.

Given that this is an urban reserve, the diversity of wildlife found here is considerable: there are some 24 mammal species, 137 recorded bird species, 22 different reptiles, seven types of frog and numerous butterfly species.

The Tiger Mountain

There are two accounts of how the 'mountain' got its name. One version is that in 1655 Jan van Riebeeck's diary refers to this area as Luipaerts Berghen (Leopard's Mountain). From a distance, the blotches visible on many Western Cape hills are reminiscent of a leopard's skin. These regular round patches are called 'heuweltjies' or small hills and are most noticeable in summer.

Some scientists think these hills are the remains of ancient termite mounds. Harvester termites drag plant material into their burrows, which, over time, changes the nature of the soil. As a result, the plants growing on these patches differ from those in surrounding areas.

Another version is that the name Tijgerberghen (Tiger Mountain) was given by settlers to the area in 1661 (early Dutch colonists referred to leopards as 'tijgers').

DURBANVILLE ROSE GARDEN

One of three trial rose gardens in the southern hemisphere

Between Durbanville Avenue and Drakenstein Road, Durbanville
Daily 7am–6pm
Free entry

Even with free entry and a prime location on one of Durbanville's main roads, many locals never visit the Durbanville Rose Garden. This is a pity, since what appears at first to be a fairly ordinary park is, in fact, home to 4,500 rose bushes of 500 different varieties, making it one of South Africa's largest collections of roses.

The garden was established in 1979 by the Western Cape Rose Society and most of the original roses were donated by enthusiasts. It's now one of three trial rose gardens in the southern hemisphere; nurseries from all over the world test their new rose varietals here.

As well as the trial plants, there are beds of medal-winning roses, collections of special antique roses, miniatures, floribundas, standards and climbing roses, alongside garden favourites such as 'Peace' and 'Mr Lincoln'.

Look out for the 'Fairest Cape' rose under the gazebo. This award-winning apricot-coloured hybrid tea rose was bred by the famous German rose breeders W Kordes & Sons in 1994, the year of South Africa's first democratic elections.

Other special roses to look out for include the large, glowing amber double blooms of 'South Africa', the superb salmon, cream and pink 'Bushveld Dawn', and the long-stemmed, bright red 'Pretoria Boys Centenary', bred by Kordes for the school's centennial celebrations in 2001. There's also the 'Dikgang Mosenke', a red David Austin rose created to honour Telkom's former chairman and former deputy chief justice of South Africa.

As you stroll around the grounds you may also notice a small graveyard. This is the family burial ground of the Schaborts, an old Cape family who leased part of their former wine estate, Eversdal, to the society.

The best time to visit the gardens is in the summer months between October and May, when most of the roses are in full bloom and their scent in the sunshine is breathtaking. On Sunday afternoons in summer, various charities serve cream teas in the tea room.

Browse and Pick Your Own Roses

Daily 9am–4.30pm
Free entry
Chart Farm on Klaassens Road in Wynberg is an 18-hectare rose farm with views over the Constantia Valley where visitors can browse and pick their own roses. Secateurs and picking trays are provided and you pay by the stem. There's also a farm stall and a coffee shop serving breakfast, lunch and teas.

ONZE MOLEN

A twin of Mostert's Mill in Durbanville

Onze Molen Road
Durbanville

At the centre of a sleepy housing estate in Durbanville stands one of Cape Town's last windmills. The mill, which was given the name Onze Molen in 1963, was originally known as Oude Molen (Old Mill), but is now the newest of the city's three remaining windmills.

In Cape Town's early years, a dozen or so windmills were built along the Liesbeek and Black Rivers, in what are now the suburbs of Pinelands, Mowbray and Salt River. The colonists used the Dutch technology to grind their wheat. As the settlement grew, the mills couldn't cope with rising demand, so more were built in outlying areas. One of these was Onze Molen in the outspan of Pampoenkraal (Pumpkin Kraal), which later became the town of Durbanville.

It's not clear exactly when or by whom the mill was built; the first definite evidence of its existence comes from a 1942 land surveyor's diagram. However, the title deed for the sale in 1843 of the farm Johannesfontein, on which it was situated, refers to the mill, so it was probably built between 1837 and 1842. The mill was used to supply local residents with flour until the early 1900s, when the roof, wings and machinery were removed and it was converted into a labourer's cottage.

The mill was eventually restored in 1983 as part of the conditions set by the city council for the subdivision of the land around it as a residential housing development. It was declared a national monument in the same year. Unfortunately, no plans for the mill were ever found, so the restoration was based on the well-known Moster's Mill in Mowbray; the two structures now look like twins.

However, Mostert's Mill was built some 50 years earlier and the restoration was criticised by South Africa's leading windmill expert, Dr James Walton, as inaccurate. Apparently, windmills built in the Cape after 1800 would not have had a thatched cap, they would have had shorter sails and been wound by a wheel and endless chain. Regrettably, residents voted against making the mill operational again due to the cost involved.

NEARBY

Pampoenkraal Fountain

Three blocks away on Hoog Street is the birthplace of Durbanville – the Pampoenkraal fontein. A small, whitewashed concrete reservoir covers two permanent springs that supply about two million litres of water a month. The springs served as the town's primary water source until 1957, when Durbanville's water-supply system was linked to Wemmershoek Dam.

ALL SAINTS CHURCH

South Africa's first female architect

2 Baxter Avenue, Durbanville
021-976-8016
Monday–Friday 9am–2pm, Sunday morning services

The charming All Saints complex, including the original church and old parsonage, as well as a hall and garden of remembrance, was designed by South Africa's first prominent female architect, Sophy Gray. The church is a white building with thatched roof, small stained-glass windows and a freestanding wooden belfry.

All Saints dates from 1859-60 and is closely associated with the history and development of the suburb of Durbanville. The original building, erected at Pampoenkraal, was a simple, rectangular structure with a nave and chancel.

By 1982 Pampoenkraal had become Durbanville and the numbers of parishioners had greatly increased. Rather than demolish and begin anew, the church was enlarged, changing it from rectangular to cruciform in shape, while sticking closely to the style of Gray's conception. Traditional methods of construction and materials were used, with old joinery retained and new joinery made to match. The church was decla-

red a national monument in 1982.

As well as an architect, Sophy Gray was a diocesan administrator, horsewoman and the wife of Cape Town bishop Robert Gray. Born on 5 January 1814 in Easington, Yorkshire, she was the fifth daughter of county squire Richard Wharton Myddleton of Durham. She died in Bishopscourt, Cape Town, on 27 April 1871 and was buried in the graveyard of St Saviour's in Claremont.

Arriving at the Cape in 1847, Robert was charged with establishing a new colonial diocese, increasing the number of clergy and building new churches and schools throughout South Africa. Sophy was his constant companion on his long travels around the country and served as both his accountant and the designer of many churches.

Before leaving England, Sophy had collected architectural plans that could be adapted for the design of churches and schools for the new Anglican parishes. Within a year of arriving at the Cape she had prepared 11 plans for small churches and over the next 25 years she designed dozens more. One of the most charming examples is All Saints.

Both Sophy and her husband favoured neo-Gothic architecture, which was all the rage in Britain at the time, but they did not stick slavishly to that style. Of more than 50 churches built in South Africa during Robert Gray's bishopric, at least 40 are attributed to Sophy.

WIJNLAND AUTO MUSEUM

An unusual and intriguing collection of motor cars

Tarentaal Street, Joostenberg Vlakte
Daily 9am–4pm

There are many people in Cape Town who've never heard of, let alone visited, the Wijnland Auto Museum, yet it's one of the most fascinating collections of vintage and classic cars you could ever hope to find.

The owner, Les Boshoff, was originally a real-estate investor who retired early and started collecting old cars as a hobby. When the film industry happened to come knocking at his door one day, he realised there was an opportunity to make his hobby pay. Since then the collection has grown to a rather staggering size. Now, 25 years later, Boshoff has more than 300 cars in various states of perfection and decay, from mint-condition Cadillacs, Buicks, Dodges and Chevrolets gleaming inside huge garages, to rows of Jaguars sagging softly under shade-cloth, to unidentifiable wrecks piled on top of one another, grass sprouting from their radiators.

The museum is on Boshoff's small-holding next to the N1 freeway in Joostenburg Vlakte. Rows of rusting hulks are visible from the road, which leads some passersby to think it's a car graveyard, yet nothing could be further from the truth. In fact, all cars at the Wijnland Auto Museum stand a chance of a glorious resurrection. Boshoff and his team are capable of turning a crumbling skeleton into a chrome and pink 60s Skoda Felicia convertible that looks like it just rolled out of the factory – all in the space of three weeks. They've supplied vehicles for many feature films shot in South Africa, driven by stars such as Colin Farrell and Salma Hayek.

They've also created convincing replicas of a land-speed-record vehicle and a Formula 1 car for advertisements. And, with the help of a French physics professor, they painstakingly converted an old Citroen DS into a replica of a unique Chapron 'Décapotable' convertible. It was then covered in yellow feathers and given a beak and wings for a Swedish advertisement for chicken.

Inside Boshoff's house are an exquisite 1923 Ford Model T Streetrod and a 1934 Ford Tallboy 3 window coupé, along with the 30-odd trophies they've won. Other venerable vehicles include a Ferrari 400i, a Porsche 356 roadster, a 1963 Rolls Royce Silver Shadow, two Ford Mustangs (as though straight out of Starsky & Hutch), and an immaculate, rare Mercedes 600, just waiting for a James Bond villain to come and give it a spin.

Car enthusiasts can spend many happy hours lost in this vehicular time-machine. The museum is also tremendously popular with photographers lucky enough to discover it.

ALPHABETICAL INDEX

Thomas Jonglez

It was September 1995 and Thomas Jonglez was in Peshawar, the northern Pakistani city 20 kilometres from the tribal zone he was to visit a few days later. It occurred to him that he should record the hidden aspects of his native city, Paris, which he knew so well. During his seven-month trip back home from Beijing, the countries he crossed took in Tibet (entering clandestinely, hidden under blankets in an overnight bus), Iran and Kurdistan. He never took a plane but travelled by boat, train or bus, hitchhiking, cycling, on horseback or on foot, reaching Paris just in time to celebrate Christmas with the family.

On his return, he spent two fantastic years wandering the streets of the capital to gather material for his first "secret guide", written with a friend. For the next seven years he worked in the steel industry until the passion for discovery overtook him. He launched Jonglez Publishing in 2003 and moved to Venice three years later.

In 2013, in search of new adventures, the family left Venice and spent six months travelling to Brazil, via North Korea, Micronesia, the Solomon Islands, Easter Island, Peru and Bolivia.

After seven years in Rio de Janeiro, he now lives in Berlin with his wife and three children.

Jonglez Publishing produces a range of titles in nine languages, released in 40 countries.

FROM THE SAME PUBLISHER

PHOTO BOOKS

Abandoned America
Abandoned Asylums
Abandoned Australia
Abandoned Churches – Unclaimed places of worship
Abandoned cinemas of the world
Abandoned France
Abandoned Italy
Abandoned Japan
Abandoned Lebanon
Abandoned Spain
Abandoned USSR
After the Final Curtain – The Fall of the American Movie Theater
After the Final Curtain – America's Abandoned Theaters
Baikonur – Vestiges of the Soviet space programme
Forbidden Places – Exploring our Abandoned Heritage Vol. 1
Forbidden Places – Exploring our Abandoned Heritage Vol. 2
Forbidden Places – Exploring our Abandoned Heritage Vol. 3
Forgotten Heritage
Oblivion
Unusual wines
Venice deserted

'SECRET' GUIDES

New York Hidden bars & restaurants
Secret Amsterdam
Secret Bali – An unusual guide
Secret Bangkok
Secret Barcelona
Secret bars & restaurants in Paris
Secret Belfast
Secret Berlin
Secret Brighton - An unusual guide
Secret Brooklyn
Secret Brussels
Secret Buenos Aires
Secret Campania
Secret Copenhagen
Secret Dublin – An unusual guide
Secret Edinburgh – An unusual guide
Secret Florence
Secret French Riviera
Secret Geneva
Secret Glasgow
Secret Granada
Secret Helsinki
Secret Istanbul
Secret Johannesburg
Secret Lisbon
Secret Liverpool – An unusual guide
Secret London – An unusual guide
Secret London – Unusual bars & restaurants

Secret Los Angeles
Secret Madrid
Secret Mexico City
Secret Milan
Secret Montreal – An unusual guide
Secret Naples
Secret New Orleans
Secret New York – An unusual guide
Secret New York – Curious activities
Secret New York – Hidden bars & restaurants
Secret Paris
Secret Prague
Secret Provence
Secret Rio
Secret Rome
Secret Seville
Secret Singapore
Secret Sussex – An unusual guide
Secret Tokyo
Secret Tuscany
Secret Venice
Secret Vienna
Secret Washington D.C.
Secret York – An unusual guide

'SOUL OF' GUIDES

Soul of Athens – A guide to 30 exceptional experiences
Soul of Barcelona – A guide to 30 exceptional experiences
Soul of Berlin – A guide to 30 exceptional experiences
Soul of Kyoto – A guide to 30 exceptional experiences
Soul of Lisbon – A guide to 30 exceptional experiences
Soul of Los Angeles – A guide to 30 exceptional experiences
Soul of Marrakesh – A guide to 30 exceptional experiences
Soul of New York – A guide to 30 exceptional experiences
Soul of Rome – A guide to 30 exceptional experiences
Soul of Tokyo – A guide to 30 exceptional experiences
Soul of Venice – A guide to 30 exceptional experiences

Follow us on Facebook, Instagram and Twitter

ACKNOWLEDGEMENTS

Special thanks to: Jonathan Price, Biddy Greene, Jana Gough, Merry Dewar, Sue Townsend

Alison Westwood :
Mark Hawthorne - Orange Kloof
Cynthia Court - City Hall Carillon
Laurenda van Breda - Cape Flats Nature Reserve
Jacques Kuyler - Blaauwberg Nature Reserve
Nicolette Nunes - Heritage Square
Rob Slater - Kenilworth Racecourse Conservation Area
Ian Walters - Casa Labia
Andre Laubscher - Tamboerskloof Farm
Peter Muller and Andrew Cochrane - Mullers Optometrists
Chin Hung Lin - Ma Tzu Temple
Bryan Little and Filipa Domingues - The Endemic Project
Ian Macfarlane - Ubuntu Wellness Centre
Jim Hislop - I Love Woodstock
Les Boshoff - Wijnland Motor Museum
Jurina Le Roux - Koeberg Nature Reserve

Justin Fox:
Richard Whiteing - Robben Island
Zainab 'Patty' Davidson - Amlay House
Tony Davenport - Josephine Mill
Christopher Peter - Irma Stern Museum
Harry Croome - Middle North gun and Martello Tower
Ryno du Rand - Tintswalo Atlantic
Anna Sala Farras - Kakapo wreck
Philip Short - Ship Society of South Africa
Jos Baker - Klein Zoar

Futher acknowledgements:
Kirk Wilhelmus, Michelle Dardagan, Susan Hayden

PHOTOGRAPHY CREDITS:
All photographs by Alison Westwood and Justin Fox except:
The Original Noon Gun: Gavin Cromhout
The Endemic Project (both images): Bryan Little
Cape Flats Nature Reserve (large image only): Laurenda van Breda
Haakgat Point (right-hand image): Tracey Younghusband

Maps: Cyrille Suss – **Layout:** Emmanuelle Willard Toulemonde – **Copy-editing:** Matt Gay and Sigrid Newman –**Proofreading:** Kimberly Bess – **Publishing:** Clémence Mathé

© JONGLEZ 2023
Registration of copyright: April 2023 – Edition: 02
ISBN: 978-2-36195-461-1
Printed in Bulgaria by Dedrax